Ultimate Snowflake Architecture for Cloud Data Warehousing

Architect, Manage, Secure, and Optimize Your Data Infrastructure Using Snowflake for Actionable Insights and Informed Decisions

Ganesh Bharathan

www.orangeava.com

First published: April 2024

Published by: Orange Education Pvt Ltd, AVA™

Address: 9, Daryaganj, Delhi, 110002, India

275 New North Road Islington Suite 1314 London,

N1 7AA, United Kingdom

ISBN: 978-81-97223-93-8

www.orangeava.com

Dedicated To

My Beloved Parents:
Padmavathi and Bharathan

My Wife and Kids:
Ambili, Meenakshi, and Nandini

My Strength and Support System

About the Author

Ganesh Bharathan holds a Master of Science in Telecommunications from George Mason University in Virginia, USA. He has over 26 years of database experience and has worked for a variety of insurance and financial companies. He began his database career with Teradata and later became a *Teradata Certified Master®* in 2008.

He has been at the forefront of his organization's cloud migration journey, leading many initiatives successfully. Ganesh is a *Snowflake Subject Matter* Expert® with many Snowflake *SnowPro Advanced certifications*, including Architect, Administrator, and Data Engineer. He also holds 17 certifications in AWS, Snowflake, Teradata, and Databricks.

Ganesh is extremely passionate about innovation, and he has been granted United States patent on "Query alerts generation for virtual warehouse" (US11494413B1), with five more pending patents approval. He has trained more than 5000 individuals in Snowflake through instructor-led courses and created several video-based training content and blogs.

He is an acclaimed tech speaker who has had the opportunity to speak at several technological conferences, including *Data Summit 2023®* and *Snowflake Summit®* three years in a row from 2022 to 2024.

Ganesh is passionate about cricket and follows the Indian cricket team. His hobbies include gardening, traveling, and learning historical information.

About the Technical Reviewers

Kumar V. Sangisetti is a Chief Data Architect, Consultant, Speaker, Trainer, and Founder of Cloud data Analytics Company DataDarwin Analytics Labs (certified partner of Snowflake, dbt, Matillion, Vaultspeed and Paradime) based in Hyderabad, India. He has over 18 years of Data Management experience with deep expertise in all aspects, from strategy, design, migrations, roadmaps, and development of Data Applications / Engineering in on-premise and cloud environments. He completed Master of Computer Applications from Osmania University and worked for TCS, Accenture and TechM as an Architect and Enterprise Architect. He is a certified professional in Snowflake, Microsoft and dbt.

Kumar excels at working with Organizational Leaders and Executives. He directs and helps them understand and break down complex data initiatives, ultimately defining how those initiatives will bring business value. He is a recognized leader in the Cloud/Data industry, often speaking at conferences and training data enthusiasts all over the world.

Vikas is a seasoned Cloud, Data and AI professional, who excels in overseeing the development, maintenance, and enhancement of robust data platforms. His expertise lies in optimizing data processing, seamless model deployment, and ensuring scalability. Vikas's strategic vision aligns with company goals and industry trends, fostering collaboration across data science, engineering, and analytics teams. He focuses on optimizing data processing, ensuring seamless model deployment, and guaranteeing scalability for the platforms. He stays at the forefront of data and AI technologies, implementing best practices and new tools to maintain a competitive edge. His key skills include proficiency in Data Engineering, AI/ML, Cybersecurity, Data Management across various platforms. He also has extensive experience in Automobiles, BFSI, Retail, Telecom, Manufacturing, and Pharma.

Acknowledgements

I express my gratitude to my parents, Mrs. Padmavathi and Mr. K.V. Bharathan, for their invaluable leadership and unwavering support. Their consistent motivation has inspired me to strive for greater achievements and pursue perfection.

My wife, Ambili, has consistently provided me with unwavering support and selflessly dedicates her time to enable me to pursue my academic aspirations. This work owes its existence to her invaluable assistance. Furthermore, I would like to express my gratitude towards my twin girls, Meenakshi and Nandini, who provide immense happiness to my life and whose unwavering affection serves as our motivation.

To my friends and colleagues with whom I have engaged in endless debates and conversations regarding various database issues, I firmly believe that knowledge expands through the act of sharing, and I have gained valuable insights from our interactions.

I would like to express my gratitude to the staff at Orange AVA for their invaluable assistance during the entire process of creating my debut book. Their support ranged from proofreading to managing the several stages of the writing process.

Preface

The Snowflake database revolutionized cloud-based databases with its unique hybrid of shared disk and shared-nothing architectures, paving the way for a rather groundbreaking approach that has become a solution for many organizations that were tied to service providers who provided a coupled compute and storage solution.

Chapter 1. Getting Started with Snowflake Architecture: This chapter provides a high-level overview of Snowflake architecture, exploring the separation of storage and computing. Snowflake handles high volume requests from concurrent users by scaling vertically and horizontally, allowing for unlimited scaling in computing and storage.

Chapter 2. Managing Organizations and Accounts: A business can have several accounts, all belonging to the central Snowflake organization. This chapter explains how to create and secure snowflake accounts in organizations. Each account is independent of the others, and we can set them up in various geographic regions, giving businesses greater flexibility.

Chapter 3. Virtual Warehouse Compute: This chapter dives into Snowflake's virtual warehouses. Snowflake was one of the first to establish the separation of compute and storage in databases with their hybrid architecture, which allowed us to consider compute on demand in the form of warehouses. Elastic computation gave us the flexibility to scale on demand.

Chapter 4. Role-Based Access Control: In this chapter, role-based access control ensures data protection at all times. Our analysis of snowflake's use of hierarchy and default roles demonstrates their effectiveness in managing roles and auditing user access.

Chapter 5. Snowflake Data Governance: Data governance is an essential component of every business, and Snowflake offers both data masking at the column level and row-based access controls at the role level. This chapter explains how to combine both of these capabilities to protect your data.

Chapter 6. Snowflake Security Framework: Snowflake native tags have numerous applications. This chapter focuses on how tags can be used to improve security and make governance easier for teams to maintain.

Chapter 7. Deployment Considerations: This chapter focuses on how Snowflake data management is done, particularly with the selection of a Snowflake region for an account and its disaster recovery strategy.

Chapter 8. Data Storage in Snowflake: Snowflake's unlimited storage and computation capability has given many enterprises the ability to grow on demand. This chapter focuses on the Snowflake data storage time travel, database clones, and data recovery.

Chapter 9. Snowflake Marketplace: The marketplace is slowly turning into a game changer for Snowflake, serving as the go-to destination for many enterprises looking for high-quality data and other marketplace services. This chapter discusses the marketplace and how it can be utilized by enterprises.

Chapter 10. Snowpark: This chapter discusses how Snowpark enables organizations to build and execute complicated data, transformations, and calculations in Snowflake using programming languages that are already familiar to users.

Get a Free eBook

We hope you are enjoying your recently purchased book! Your feedback is incredibly valuable to us, and to all other readers looking for great books.

If you found this book helpful or enjoyable, we would truly appreciate it, if you could take a moment to leave a short review with a 5 star rating on Amazon. It helps us grow, and lets other readers discover our books.

As a thank you, we would love to send you a free digital copy of this book, and a **30%** discount code on your next cart value on our official websites:

www.orangeava.com

www.orangeava.in (For Indian Subcontinent)

☑ **Here's how:**

Leave a review for the book on Amazon.

Take a screenshot of your review, and send an email to **info@orangeava.com** (it can be just the confirmation screen).

Once, we receive your screenshot, we will send you the digital file, within 24 hours.

Thank you so much for your support – it means a lot to us!

Colored Images

Please follow the links or scan the QR codes to download the
Images of the book:

You can find code bundles of our books on our official Github Repository. Go to the following link to and QR code to explore the further:

https://github.com/orgs/ava-orange-education/repositories

Please follow the link to download the Colored Images of the book:
https://rebrand.ly/586d05

In case there's an update to the code, it will be updated on the existing GitHub repository.

Errata

We take immense pride in our work at **Orange Education Pvt Ltd,** and follow best practices to ensure the accuracy of our content to provide an indulging reading experience to our subscribers. Our readers are our mirrors, and we use their inputs to reflect and improve upon human errors, if any, that may have occurred during the publishing processes involved. To let us maintain the quality and help us reach out to any readers who might be having difficulties due to any unforeseen errors, please write to us at :

errata@orangeava.com

Your support, suggestions, and feedback are highly appreciated.

DID YOU KNOW

Did you know that Orange Education Pvt Ltd offers eBook versions of every book published, with PDF and ePub files available? You can upgrade to the eBook version at **www.orangeava.com** and as a print book customer, you are entitled to a discount on the eBook copy. Get in touch with us at: **info@orangeava.com** for more details.

At **www.orangeava.com**, you can also read a collection of free technical articles, sign up for a range of free newsletters, and receive exclusive discounts and offers on AVA™ Books and eBooks.

PIRACY

If you come across any illegal copies of our works in any form on the internet, we would be grateful if you would provide us with the location address or website name. Please contact us at **info@orangeava.com** with a link to the material.

ARE YOU INTERESTED IN AUTHORING WITH US?

If there is a topic that you have expertise in, and you are interested in either writing or contributing to a book, please write to us at **business@orangeava.com**. We are on a journey to help developers and tech professionals to gain insights on the present technological advancements and innovations happening across the globe and build a community that believes Knowledge is best acquired by sharing and learning with others. Please reach out to us to learn what our audience demands and how you can be part of this educational reform. We also welcome ideas from tech experts and help them build learning and development content for their domains.

REVIEWS

Please leave a review. Once you have read and used this book, why not leave a review on the site that you purchased it from? Potential readers can then see and use your unbiased opinion to make purchase decisions. We at Orange Education would love to know what you think about our products, and our authors can learn from your feedback. Thank you!

For more information about Orange Education, please visit **www.orangeava.com**.

Table of Contents

CHAPTER 1

Getting Started With Snowflake Architecture

Introduction

Welcome to the world of Snowflake, a cutting-edge cloud-based database designed to transform how businesses manage their data. This chapter will guide you through the fundamentals of Snowflake's architecture and how it sets the foundations for scalable, flexible, and high-performance data processing platforms.

Snowflake's design distinguishes itself through its new approach to separating computing and storage, a paradigm change that provides significant benefits over standard data warehousing systems. We will investigate how Snowflake's decoupled architecture enables businesses to handle enormous data volumes without sacrificing performance or paying excessive costs as we embark on this trip.

In this chapter, we will look at the fundamental components of Snowflake's architecture, focusing on the interaction between its storage layer, where data is safely kept in an encryption mode and managed, and its compute layer, which is in charge of executing queries and analytical operations. We will look at the flexibility of virtual warehouse provisioning and how this separation allows you to scale computing resources on-demand, resulting in the best resource use.

Join us as we unravel the intricacies of Snowflake's architecture, learning how this unique design not only meets a wide range of business requirements but also paves the way for seamless data integration, and rapid querying, and helps make quick data-driven decision-making. This chapter will provide you with the foundational information you need to make the most of Snowflake's robust architecture.

Structure

In this chapter, the following topics to be covered:

- Three Important Layers of Snowflake's Architecture
- Separation of Compute and Storage
- Scaling Up for Large Workloads
- Handling Multiple Concurrent Users

Introduction to Snowflake Architecture

Traditional database architecture typically provides two options: shared disk and shared nothing. The main difference is how data is stored and accessed across multiple nodes, which is the most important difference between these approaches.

Multiple nodes in a distributed system share a single disk on which data is stored, according to the shared-disk architecture. Each node has its own memory and processing capacity but simultaneously accesses the shared disk. Since every node can directly access the data, this architecture provides high data availability. It also facilitates the sharing of data between nodes, as they can read and write to the shared disk without explicit communication. However, contention issues can arise in shared-disk architectures when multiple nodes simultaneously attempt to access the same disk. This contention can result in obstacles to performance and diminished scalability.

The shared-nothing architecture, on the other hand, allocates dedicated disks to each system node. Each node has its own disk, memory, and processing capacity, allowing it to operate independently from other nodes. In this method, data is distributed across nodes, with each node managing and processing its own portion of data. Adding more nodes to this architecture does not necessitate sharing resources or coordinating access to a shared disk, thereby enhancing scalability and fault tolerance. However, in a shared-nothing architecture, sharing data between nodes requires explicit communication and coordination, making it more difficult to implement.

The decision between shared-disk and shared-nothing architectures is influenced by a number of variables, including performance requirements, data sharing patterns, and fault tolerance requirements. Shared-disk architectures are typically preferred for read-intensive workloads with high data-sharing requirements, whereas shared-nothing architectures are favored for write-intensive workloads that prioritize scalability and defect tolerance.

Snowflake is a modern cloud-based data platform that employs a proprietary architecture known as multi-cluster shared data. This technique enables numerous compute clusters to simultaneously access and process the same underlying data, ensuring scalability and high-performance analytics.

Snowflake divides storage and compute layers in the multi-cluster shared data architecture. The data is kept in Snowflake Storage, a highly scalable and durable storage layer, while the compute layer is made up of independent virtual warehouses or clusters. These computing clusters can scale independently to meet processing demands and can access and query the shared data stored in Snowflake Storage in real-time.

This architecture has numerous advantages. Multiple compute clusters can operate on the same dataset at the same time, enabling parallel processing and improving performance. Without any data duplication or synchronization overhead, the data remains consistent and accessible to all compute clusters. It also offers automatic data optimization, allowing query execution to be offloaded to the best compute cluster based on data placement and workload.

Three Important Layers of Snowflake's Architecture

The architecture of Snowflake is made up of three major layers: the cloud services layer, the virtual warehouse layer, and the storage layer. This multi-layered architecture is intended to provide scalability, flexibility, and performance when dealing with large-scale data processing and analytics workloads.

The cloud services layer serves as the Snowflake system's control plane. Services such as metadata management, query optimization, security, and transaction management are included. This layer coordinates and manages all system processes, guaranteeing effective resource allocation and task management. This layer also checks for user authentication and user access to data via role-based access control.

Figure 1.1 shows the three layers of Snowflake's architecture:

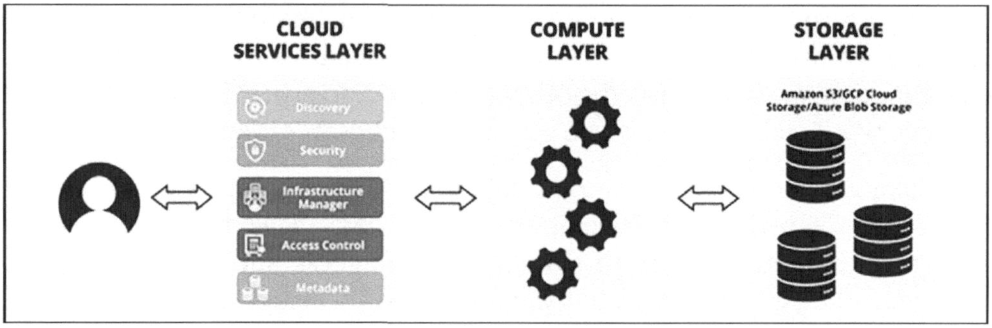

Figure 1.1: *Three Layers of Snowflake Architecture*

The computational resources are located in the virtual warehouse layer. It is made up of a number of virtual warehouses, which are compute clusters that execute queries and perform analytical operations. Each virtual warehouse can be scaled individually, allowing users to assign computing power based on their workload demands. This layer allows for parallel processing and concurrent access to shared data.

Snowflake Storage, the storage layer, is in charge of data persistence and durability. It makes use of an improved columnar storage format and compression techniques to reduce storage requirements while increasing query performance. Snowflake Storage data is automatically partitioned and structured to allow for efficient query execution. Furthermore, Snowflake's distinct architecture enables the storage and computation layers to scale separately, allowing for greater flexibility in managing storage capacity and computing resources.

Snowflake is able to provide various benefits due to its three-layered architecture. Users may increase computation resources independently of data storage thanks to the separation of compute and storage, which provides cost optimization and elastic scalability. The shared data paradigm maintains data consistency and eliminates data silos, making data sharing and collaboration across computing clusters simple. Snowflake's architecture also includes innovative query optimization algorithms and automated indexing, which improve query efficiency and accelerate analytical operations.

Separation of Compute and Storage

The separation of compute and storage is one of Snowflake's fundamental architectural features, which provides the most benefits in terms of scalability, performance, and cost optimization. Snowflake's architecture decouples computation and storage resources, allowing them to scale and be controlled independently.

Snowflake's separation of computing and storage provides various advantages. It offers elastic scalability and users can quickly scale up or down their computational capacity based on workload demands, without worrying about data migration or duplication. This elasticity enables organizations to handle peak demands in a cost-effective and efficient manner.

Another advantage is the ability to separate storage and computation costs. Because Snowflake bills computing and storage separately, users only pay for the compute resources they utilize, without incurring additional fees for data storage. This decoupling allows for greater cost management flexibility and alignment with real usage.

The separation of CPU and storage improves performance as well. Snowflake's storage layer is optimized for high-performance analytics. It makes use of a columnar storage structure and compression algorithms to provide fast data retrieval and query execution. Snowflake can give quick and scalable performance by leveraging the capabilities of parallel processing and distributed computing with compute resources dedicated to query processing and analytics.

Additionally, the separation of compute and storage allows for data sharing and collaboration. Multiple compute clusters can access and query the same underlying data at the same time without data migration or duplication. This shared data facilitates cooperation and eliminates the need for data replication or synchronization by simplifying data sharing among various teams or users.

Overall, Snowflake's separation of computing and storage gives enterprises flexibility, scalability, performance, and cost optimization. It enables customers to scale computational resources independently of data storage, resulting in elastic scalability and resource utilization. The shared data paradigm allows for seamless collaboration and data sharing, increasing productivity and removing data silos.

Scaling Up for Large Workloads

With its scalable architecture, Snowflake, the data cloud technology, excels at handling massive workloads. Because of the architecture's design, businesses can quickly scale up their resources to meet the needs of massive data processing, providing optimal performance and cost-effectiveness.

The scalable design of Snowflake is based on the separation of computing and storage. The storage layer, which makes use of object storage services such as Amazon S3 or Microsoft Azure Blob Storage, enables the efficient and elastic storage of large amounts of data. This separation reduces the need to allocate additional storage resources when increasing computation capacity, allowing for greater agility in managing data expansion.

When dealing with massive workloads, Snowflake provides a one-of-a-kind capability known as virtual warehouses. Virtual warehouses are computational resource clusters that may be provisioned and scaled on demand. Snowflake's separation of computation and storage allows customers to allocate compute resources independently without affecting the underlying data storage. Because of this decoupling, enterprises may easily increase compute power to manage enormous workloads and improve query performance.

Snowflake's design is based on a shared-nothing, multi-cluster paradigm, as mentioned earlier. This architecture enables parallel query processing over numerous computing nodes within a virtual warehouse, resulting in significant performance improvements for data-intensive tasks. Snowflake dynamically scales compute resources as workloads grow in size by adding more compute nodes, ensuring efficient query execution and minimal latency.

Snowflake's capacity to scale up for enormous workloads is also aided by its transparent and intelligent optimization capabilities. The query optimizer in Snowflake uses complicated algorithms and analytics to optimize query execution plans, ensuring effective resource use and decreasing query processing time even with big datasets.

Several enterprises have discovered the advantages of using Snowflake to scale up for enormous workloads. Many global technology firms adopted Snowflake's design to meet their high-volume data analytics requirements. They realized considerable speed improvements and the capacity to handle peak workloads without interruptions by employing Snowflake's scalable compute resources.

Snowflake's design provides a solid foundation for scaling up to efficiently handle big workloads. The flexibility to offer virtual warehouses on-demand, together with the separation of computation and storage, enables enterprises to grow their resources elastically, assuring optimal performance and cost-effective data processing.

Handling Multiple Concurrent Users

Snowflake's architecture is designed to efficiently handle several concurrent users, ensuring excellent performance and easy data processing. Snowflake delivers a scalable and shared environment that responds to the needs of several users accessing data at the same time, thanks to its innovative approach to separating computing and storage.

The separation of compute and storage is a major feature of Snowflake's design that also enables effective handling of concurrent users. Data is kept in a scalable and persistent storage layer, such as Amazon S3 or Microsoft Azure Blob Storage, while computational resources are provided as virtual warehouses independently. Due to this separation, computing resources may be scaled independently based on the number of concurrent users and their query demands.

Snowflake virtual warehouses are in charge of executing queries and analytical processes. They can be dynamically provisioned, allowing companies to deploy the right number of compute resources to accommodate concurrent user workload. The auto-scaling functionality in Snowflake automatically adjusts the number of compute nodes within a virtual warehouse based on the incoming query workload, providing optimal performance and resource use.

Shared-nothing paradigm in Snowflake's design is key in its concurrency handling also, with each virtual warehouse operating independently. This means that several users can run queries across separate virtual warehouses at the same time without interfering with each other's performance. Because of this architecture, each user's requests are performed individually and in parallel, resulting in efficient query execution and low latency.

Snowflake also has powerful concurrency controls for managing and prioritizing query execution among numerous concurrent users. It makes use of a query scheduling and execution architecture that handles resource allocation dynamically and assures equitable access to compute resources. This technique prioritizes vital requests, avoiding resource contention and guaranteeing that all users receive timely query results. We will cover this extensively in our warehouse chapter.

The capacity to handle several concurrent users efficiently is critical for data-driven companies. In this aspect, many businesses have reaped the benefits of Snowflake's architecture. For example, Snowflake was used by DoorDash, a leading food delivery business, to manage its growing user base and demanding data analytics requirements. DoorDash was able to accommodate concurrent users accessing and analyzing data in real-time because of Snowflake's scalable design, which aided their decision-making processes and improved consumer experiences.

Snowflake's design excels at supporting numerous concurrent users by detaching computing and storage, enabling independent scalability of compute resources, leveraging a shared-nothing approach, and implementing effective concurrency controls. Snowflake is a strong platform for enterprises dealing with enormous user bases and heavy data workloads since this strategy assures optimal performance, minimal latency, and equitable resource distribution.

Industry Applications

Snowflake has transformed multiple sectors through the provision of a highly adaptable and scalable data platform that operates in the cloud. Snowflake empowers financial institutions to efficiently handle and analyze large volumes of data, hence assisting in risk management, fraud detection, and regulatory compliance.

Snowflake enables the secure and compliant storage of patient data, promotes advanced analytics for tailored medicine, and simplifies data sharing among healthcare providers. Snowflake assists retail establishments in examining customer behavior, optimizing inventory management, and improving the entire customer experience by providing individualized recommendations.

Conclusion

In summary, Snowflake's architecture transforms the way businesses organize and process data. Snowflake allows scalable, flexible, and high-performance data processing by separating compute and storage. The separation of compute and storage enables autonomous resource scaling, which optimizes cost management and resource use. Furthermore, because of its parallel processing capabilities, Snowflake's shared-nothing approach allows several concurrent users to access and process data without affecting performance. Snowflake's sophisticated concurrency controls prioritize queries and efficiently manage resources, ensuring fair access and responsive query responses for all users.

Because of its elastic scalability and intelligent query optimization, Snowflake's design has proven to be useful for handling big workloads. Businesses may quickly scale up compute resources to handle enormous workloads without compromising performance or incurring extra storage expenditures. Another feature of Snowflake's design is its capacity to manage several concurrent users, providing a shared environment in which users may access and analyze data in real-time without contention.

Snowflake's architecture has benefited numerous enterprises, including faster query performance, increased scalability, and easier data processing. Snowflake's architecture has been used by companies to handle their growing user base and complicated analytics requirements, allowing them to make data-driven choices and improve consumer experiences.

Snowflake's adaptability is particularly evident in cutting-edge applications, such as data research and artificial intelligence (AI). The platform's seamless integration with Snowpark, a native JavaScript data programming language, enables data scientists to immediately do intricate analytics within the platform. The Snowflake Marketplace provides a diverse range of data-driven solutions, promoting creativity and cooperation. The Snowflake in Snowflake (SiS) methodology guarantees a straightforward and precise process for sharing and exchanging data. Snowflake plays a crucial role in facilitating progress at the convergence of technology and analytics as firms adapt to the changing data world.

In conclusion, the Snowflake architecture provides the foundation for scalable, flexible, and high-performance data processing. Its separation of computing and storage, shared-nothing model, and concurrency enable it to handle big workloads and several concurrent users efficiently. Businesses may unlock the full potential of their data and speed up their data-driven decision-making processes by implementing Snowflake's architecture.

In the next chapter, you will learn about the fundamental components of Snowflake's organization and accounts. Discover how these critical components influence data management, access control, and resource allocation. Learn how to optimize your Snowflake organization to meet your firm's increasing data needs.

References

- https://www.geeksforgeeks.org/difference-between-shared-nothing-architecture-and-shared-disk-architecture/
- https://docs.snowflake.com/en/user-guide/intro-key-concepts#multi-cluster-shared-data-architecture
- https://www.snowflake.com/en/resources/case-study/doordash-maximizes-the-power-of-data-and-bi-with-snowflake/

CHAPTER 2

Managing Organizations and Accounts

Introduction

Data has become the cornerstone of decision-making, growth, and innovation in today's fast-changing business scene. To fully realize the value of data, businesses must have a solid data management platform that not only allows for easy collaboration and safe access, but also allows for scalability and compliance with regulatory standards. Snowflake, a cutting-edge cloud data platform, provides a comprehensive set of functionality designed to meet these important requirements.

This chapter digs into the critical components that enable businesses to realize the full value of their data inside the Snowflake ecosystem. Snowflake Organizations, Accounts, Regions, and Security are four critical components that contribute to Snowflake's unrivaled data management capabilities.

As a significant element of the Snowflake Data Cloud, Snowflake Organizations offer an organized approach to data administration, collaboration, and safe access across numerous accounts. Organizations improve data governance, control, and sharing by developing hierarchical frameworks, while also streamlining data access for seamless collaboration.

Snowflake's core building pieces, accounts, play a critical role in data separation, scalability, and security. We'll go over the importance of the `orgadmin` role in generating new accounts, as well as how a consistent naming pattern allows easy management and identification.

Enterprises may maximize data residency, performance, and compliance by strategically selecting Snowflake Regions. Understanding the significance of regions in Snowflake enables businesses to manage their data strategically across different geographic locations while adhering to data governance rules.

Snowflake's rigorous security features have earned it a reputation for securing sensitive data, which is the backbone of every data-driven enterprise. We will examine a range of security features that increase data protection and reduce the danger of unwanted access, ranging from federated authentication and Single Sign-On (SSO) to Multi-Factor Authentication (MFA) and SCIM.

As we progress through these related themes, it becomes clear that Snowflake provides a comprehensive and integrated framework for successful data management, allowing businesses to prosper in a data-centric environment. Organizations may unleash the full potential of their data, encourage collaboration, achieve scalability, and assure the highest levels of security by following the insights and best practices discussed in this chapter. Let's go on this adventure to discover the revolutionary potential of Snowflake's data management skills.

Structure

In this chapter, the following topics will be covered:

- Snowflake Organization
- Snowflake Accounts
- Snowflake Regions
- Account Security

Snowflake Organization

Snowflake Organization is an important feature within the Snowflake Data Cloud that was created to enable data administration, collaboration, and safe access across various accounts. It makes it possible for businesses to set up a hierarchical structure, which improves data governance and control while also making accessing and sharing data much easier. In this overview, we will investigate how a new business might establish a new organization by making use of the `orgadmin` role. Particular attention will be paid to name standards, security issues, and how this architecture facilitates future account sharing and replications. In addition, we will discuss how Organization Usage Information effectively and efficiently communicates vital data between accounts.

To create a new organization, a user needs to have the **orgadmin** role. Those with the **orgadmin** role are granted administrative privileges within the organization. These privileges provide them the ability to successfully create accounts and regulate resources. When assigned the **orgadmin** role, individuals immediately gain full control over the organization's policy framework and organizational structure.

Naming Convention and the Security of the **OrgAdmin** Role is vital to establish a clear and consistent naming convention for accounts, users, and other objects when creating a new organization. This naming convention ensures clarity and simplicity within the organization, making it easier to recognize and manage the various entities that exist within it. A naming convention should be straightforward and uncomplicated, avoiding the use of esoteric terminology and abbreviations whenever possible.

When it comes to protecting sensitive information and preventing unwanted access, the security of the **orgadmin** role is of the utmost significance. The **orgadmin** role should be reserved for only the most reliable members of the organization, and multi-factor authentication should be required to add an additional layer of security. To keep the environment secure and reduce the likelihood of data being stolen or otherwise compromised, regular security audits and access reviews must be carried out.

Snowflake is the design that will be used for future account shares and replications. Organizations are built to make future account sharing and replications easier, simplifying the process of working together across multiple accounts. The establishment of a hierarchical structure enables businesses to efficiently manage and communicate data between parent accounts and their children's accounts. This design simplifies granting access to multiple accounts and also enables smooth replication and sharing of data.

Figure 2.1 depicts how snowflake accounts are located in a snowflake region and how all these accounts scattered across regions complete an organization's snowflake:

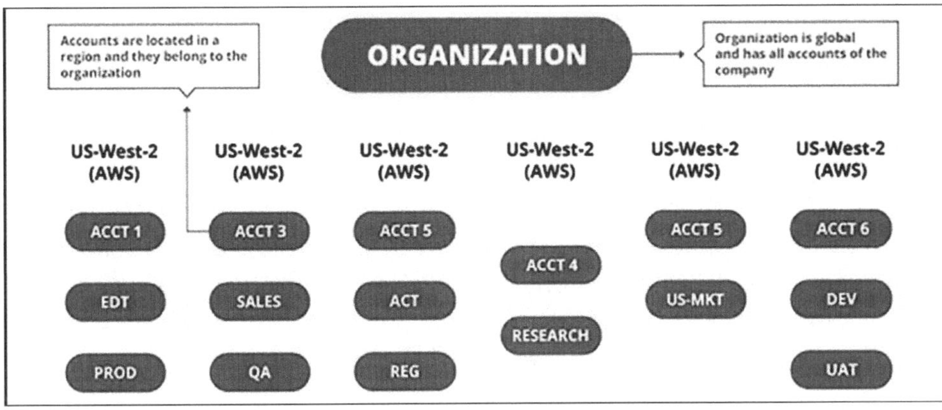

Figure 2.1: *Snowflake Organization Structure*

The Sharing Organization Level Information feature of Organization Usage Information allows crucial use data to be shared between accounts that are part of an organization. It provides extremely helpful insights into the utilization of resources, query performance, and overall data usage. As this information is shared across accounts, businesses can optimize their resource utilization, pinpoint areas experiencing bottlenecks, and guarantee effective data processing.

Snowflake Organizations deliver an effective and safe method for businesses to collaborate on data management across different accounts within the Snowflake Data Cloud, resulting in time and money saving. When forming a new organization, a new corporation can set a clear naming standard for the organization by selecting an **`orgadmin`** role, ensuring that the organization's naming standard is simple and consistent. Protecting sensitive data and preventing unauthorized access to the **`orgadmin`** role requires the implementation of appropriate security measures.

The organizational structure of hierarchical companies makes it possible to easily share and replicate accounts in the future, promoting collaboration and smooth data exchange. Additionally, Organization Usage Information guarantees efficient transmission of vital data on resource use and query performance between accounts. This enables businesses to optimize their resource utilization and increase their overall data processing capabilities.

Snowflake organizations play an essential part in enabling effective data management and promoting cooperation across the enterprise, which is becoming increasingly important as businesses place a greater emphasis on data-driven decision-making. Organizations can exploit Snowflake's capabilities to unleash the full potential of their data and drive the growth and innovation of their businesses if the appropriate governance, security, and design considerations are applied.

Snowflake Accounts

Snowflake Accounts are also critical components of the Snowflake Data Cloud architecture, offering enterprises with data separation, scalability, and increased security. In this section, we will look at the concept of Snowflake Accounts, covering how to establish new accounts with the **`orgadmin`** role and the significance of naming standards. We'll also examine the **`accountadmin`** role, security concerns, and the sharing of account usage data. In addition, we will also go over the distinctions between Snowflake Accounts and Snowflake Organizations, as well as the significance of Snowflake Regions.

The **`orgadmin`** role is necessary for creating new accounts in Snowflake. The **`orgadmin`** has administrative rights within the organization and has the ability to create and manage accounts. This role ensures that accounts are properly configured and governed, allowing companies to successfully manage their data and resources. New accounts can be established and provisioned with the relevant settings and permissions by leveraging the **`orgadmin`** role.

Establishing a uniform and relevant naming pattern for accounts is critical for clarity, structure, and simplicity of management. A well-defined name convention should adhere to a logical structure and include pertinent information such as the account's purpose, the department or team affiliated with it, or any other important identifier. A consistent name strategy makes account identification and management easier, especially as the number of accounts inside an organization grows.

The **`accountadmin`** role has account-level administrative privileges and is in charge of managing user access, security settings, and resource allocation within a given account. The **`accountadmin`** role guarantees that the correct individual has the authority to govern and control the resources and data in an account. To ensure the account's security and integrity, only trusted personnel should be granted the **`accountadmin`** role. Multi-factor authentication and frequent security audits should also be implemented to improve the account's security posture.

Sharing Account Usage Information is a useful tool that allows you to share detailed usage data at the account level. It gives enterprises insights into resource utilization, query performance, and data consumption, allowing them to optimize their resources, discover usage patterns, and assure effective data processing. This data is critical for capacity planning, performance optimization, and cost control.

Snowflake Organizations provide a hierarchical structure for managing multiple accounts, while Snowflake Accounts represent individual instances inside the organization. Accounts allow companies to segment their data and manage access and rights at the account level, and on the other hand, Organizations provide a broader structure for account management, allowing for smooth collaboration and data exchange between parent and child accounts. Accounts are the foundation of Organizations, providing granular control over data and resources.

Snowflake Regions

Snowflake Regions play an important role in the design of Snowflake's cloud data platform, allowing enterprises to manage their data strategically across multiple geographic locations. In this section, we will look at the notion of Snowflake Regions, their relevance, and how businesses can use them efficiently.

Snowflake Regions are physical locations that house Snowflake's cloud architecture. Each location has various availability zones to ensure high availability and data durability. Snowflake offers a worldwide footprint with regions spread across multiple geographic locations, allowing enterprises to select the most appropriate region(s) for their specific needs.

Snowflake Regions enable enterprises to comply with data residency and compliance laws. Organizations must comply with particular data sovereignty or residency rules in different regions. Organizations can ensure that their data remains within the required geographical boundaries by selecting the right region(s), thereby following regulatory obligations and data governance rules.

Selecting the appropriate Snowflake Region can have a major influence on performance and user experience. Organizations can reduce latency and obtain faster query response times by choosing an area that is geographically proximate to their users or data sources. The proximity of data to consumers reduces network latency and assures optimal performance, boosting overall data processing and analytics capabilities.

Snowflake's multi-region design with availability zones guarantees high availability and disaster recovery capabilities. Within a region, availability zones are physically different data centers with autonomous power, cooling, and network equipment. This configuration provides redundancy and fault tolerance, ensuring data accessibility even if a localized failure or disruption occurs. Organizations can replicate their data across different regions for increased robustness, allowing for seamless failover and operation continuity.

Snowflake Regions make data replication and worldwide data sharing easier. Data replication allows organizations to replicate data from one region to another, allowing remote data processing, redundancy, and business continuity. Organizations can use this replication to build global data pipelines, transfer data across regions, and facilitate multi-region analytics and reporting. It promotes data-driven decision-making on a global scale by enabling cooperation across teams and stakeholders in diverse geographical areas.

Snowflake Regions provide enterprises with the flexibility and scalability they require. Organizations can select areas based on their business requirements, client base, and compliance constraints. Organizations may simply scale their operations as their business grows or new markets arise by provisioning extra resources or moving into new locations within the Snowflake ecosystem. This adaptability enables businesses to effectively harness the benefits of cloud computing while adapting to changing demands.

Snowflake Regions enable enterprises to manage their data strategically across multiple geographic locations. Companies can assure data residency compliance, optimize performance, and improve data availability and disaster recovery capabilities by selecting the proper region(s). Snowflake Regions also provide data replication, worldwide data exchange, and scalability, allowing enterprises to effectively exploit their data assets and create business success in a quickly expanding digital landscape.

Snowflake Accounts form the foundation of the Snowflake Data Cloud, enabling data segregation, scalability, and better security. Organizations can use the **`orgadmin`** role to create and manage accounts, ensuring proper configuration and control. Using a consistent naming pattern makes account administration and identification easier.

The **`accountadmin`** role regulates account-level user access, security settings, and resource distribution, boosting security and control. Account Utilization Sharing information provides useful insights into resource utilization and data consumption, allowing for optimization and cost management.

Snowflake Accounts and Snowflake Organizations collaborate to make data administration and collaboration easier. Organizations provide a hierarchical structure for managing multiple accounts and enabling data sharing, whereas accounts provide data isolation. Snowflake Regions give enterprises the freedom to choose the best geographical location for their needs.

Organizations may obtain effective data management, scalability, and increased security by employing Snowflake Accounts within the Snowflake Data Cloud, ultimately empowering them to harness the full potential of their data for corporate growth and innovation.

Account Security

Because corporations manage massive volumes of data, protecting the security of their databases is critical. Snowflake, a popular cloud data platform, provides several powerful security features to protect data and ensure a safe user experience. In this section, we will look at Snowflake's database security mechanisms, such as Federated Authentication and Single Sign-On (SSO), Multi-Factor Authentication (MFA), Snowflake Network Policy, and System for Cross-domain Identity Management (SCIM). We'll look at how these features improve Snowflake's security and enable enterprises to properly protect their data.

Federated Authentication allows users to access Snowflake databases using their existing identity provider (IdP) credentials. Snowflake works as a service provider (SP) in Federated Authentication, relying on external identity providers to authenticate users. Centralizing authentication controls eliminates the need for separate Snowflake-specific passwords, streamlines user management, and improves security. SSO enhances the user experience by allowing users to access numerous applications, including Snowflake, with a single set of credentials.

MFA adds an extra layer of protection by demanding users to give several forms of verification before accessing Snowflake databases. This is usually something the person knows (like a password), something they have (like a mobile device), or something they are (like biometric data). MFA improves authentication, reduces the risk of unwanted access, and safeguards sensitive data even if credentials are compromised.

Snowflake Network Policy enables enterprises to create network-level access controls to their Snowflake databases. This feature allows administrators to establish and implement detailed network traffic management policies, ensuring that only approved connections are allowed. Network Policy enables enterprises to restrict access to Snowflake deployments based on IP addresses, virtual private clouds (VPCs), or specified network ranges, offering an extra layer of protection.

AWS PrivateLink enables secure connectivity to services within your VPC without the need for public internet access. Snowflake enables the use of AWS PrivateLink to provide secure and private communication between your Snowflake account and an AWS VPC.

SCIM is a standard protocol that allows for automatic user provisioning and maintenance across different platforms. SCIM compatibility in Snowflake enables enterprises to synchronize user information and access controls between Snowflake and their identity management systems. SCIM allows for the automation of user provisioning and de-provisioning, minimizing manual overhead, ensuring consistency, and boosting security by swiftly removing access for terminated users.

Snowflake improves database security and provides strong protection against unwanted access and data breaches by integrating these security elements. Organizations can implement a complete security strategy that meets their specific needs. Snowflake also includes detailed audit logs, allowing enterprises to monitor user actions and follow changes to database configurations.

It is important to note that, while Snowflake provides a safe platform, the company is responsible for implementing security controls and best practices. This involves enforcing strong passwords, regularly monitoring access controls, and conducting security audits to detect and remedy potential vulnerabilities.

Finally, Snowflake's database security capabilities, such as Federated Authentication and SSO, MFA, Snowflake Network Policy, and SCIM, enable enterprises to reinforce their data protection methods. These features improve user authentication, regulate network access, automate user administration, and offer extensive auditing capabilities. By leveraging these security safeguards, organizations can store and manage their data on Snowflake with confidence, knowing that their databases are protected by industry-leading security features.

Conclusion

Snowflake Organizations and Accounts are important components of the Snowflake Data Cloud, allowing organizations to manage data, collaborate, and gain secure access across multiple accounts. Organizations provide a hierarchical framework that improves data governance and control, allowing more efficient data sharing and access. To create a new organization, users must have the orgadmin role, which grants administrative powers over user access, account creation, and resource management. A clear naming convention, as well as strong security mechanisms like multi-factor authentication and security audits, protect data and prevent unauthorized access to the orgadmin role.

Snowflake's design makes future account sharing and replications easier, allowing firms to effortlessly transfer data between parent and child accounts. The Sharing Organization Usage Information feature gives enterprises significant insights into resource consumption, query performance, and data usage, allowing them to efficiently improve their data processing and resource allocation.

Snowflake Accounts serve as the backbone of the Snowflake Data Cloud, offering data isolation, scalability, and better security. For clarity and convenience of management, organizations can utilize the `orgadmin` role to create and manage accounts while adhering to a uniform naming pattern. Sharing account usage information provides valuable insights for optimizing resource consumption, and the `accountadmin` job allows account-level administrative access.

Snowflake Regions are critical components of the data platform, allowing organizations to manage their data strategically across multiple geographic locations. By selecting the right region(s), organizations can comply with data residency and compliance rules. The right region also plays an important role in performance, as proximity reduces latency and ensures faster query response times. Snowflake's multi-region design ensures high availability and disaster recovery, allowing for data replication and global data sharing.

Federated Authentication and Single Sign-On (SSO), Multi-Factor Authentication (MFA), Snowflake Network Policy, and SCIM are used to strengthen Snowflake Database Security. Federated Authentication makes user administration easier by centralizing authentication controls, whereas MFA increases security by demanding several kinds of verification. Snowflake Network Policy allows for network-level access controls, limiting connections to authorized sources. SCIM enables automatic user provisioning and de-provisioning, reducing manual overhead and ensuring platform consistency.

Snowflake Organizations and Accounts, together with Snowflake Regions and comprehensive database security features, enable organizations to effectively manage their data, boost collaboration, and assure data security across the Snowflake Data Cloud. Organizations may capture the full potential of their data for growth and innovation by exploiting these qualities in an increasingly data-driven environment.

In the next chapter, we will look at the snowflake warehouse, the most important component of the snowflake database. This warehouse provides a flexible and elastic computing environment for query execution, allowing organizations to manage duties of varying sizes and complexities with ease.

CHAPTER 3

Virtual Warehouse Compute

Introduction

The capacity to efficiently and effectively handle huge volumes of data is critical in the ever-changing landscape of data management and analytics. Data warehousing solutions have become essential for firms trying to maximize the value of their data. Snowflake, a cloud-based data warehousing technology known for its scalability and performance, is a market leader in this field. One of the key elements that contributes to Snowflake's strength is its ability to scale both up and out, allowing organizations to effortlessly adjust to changing data demands.

Scaling up, also known as vertical scaling, is the process of expanding the computational capabilities of a single server or node. In the context of Snowflake, this involves adding extra resources to a virtual warehouse or cluster, like CPU and memory. This method is excellent for situations in which a single query or job demands significant processing power but is not necessarily dispersed over numerous nodes. Snowflake allows enterprises to resize virtual warehouses with a simple change, allowing them to respond to fluctuating workloads in real-time. This method is very effective when dealing with complicated analytical queries because it allows Snowflake to allocate more resources to the work at hand, resulting in faster query execution.

Scaling out, also known as horizontal scaling, entails adding extra nodes to a distributed system. This involves creating more virtual warehouses or clusters to work concurrently in Snowflake. When dealing with large-scale data processing requirements, scaling out is the preferred approach. Each extra node contributes processing power, allowing Snowflake to handle several queries at the same time. This method improves Snowflake's ability to manage enormous data volumes while also providing greater performance for workloads that require parallelism. It is especially useful for dealing with scenarios such as data loading, ETL procedures, and concurrent user requests since it helps Snowflake to optimally spread the workload.

We will go deeper into the benefits and considerations of scaling up and scaling out in this discussion of Snowflake's scaling methodologies. We will look at scenarios where each technique excels and offer advice on how to make informed judgments to fit your organization's specific data warehousing needs. Whether you're dealing with small datasets or petabytes of data, understanding how Snowflake's scaling capabilities may optimize your data operations is critical to realizing the full potential of this powerful platform.

Structure

In this chapter, the following topics to be covered:

- Snowflake Query's Lifecycle
- Selecting the Optimal Warehouse Size and Number of Clusters
- Scaling Strategy, Query Timeouts, and Maximum Mode to Optimize Snowflake Costs
- Types of Warehouses
- Snowflake Features that Improve Query Performance
- Warehouse Cache and Query Cache

Snowflake Query's Lifecycle

Queries in Snowflake follow an exclusive robust architecture that lets them begin and end in the same virtual warehouse-size cluster. This implies that when you launch a query, it begins execution in the virtual warehouse of your choice at the size you specify, and it continues in that warehouse until completion, even if you modify the warehouse size while the query is running. We'll go through this feature in-depth and explain its benefits.

When a user submits a query in Snowflake, they select and specify the size of a virtual warehouse for execution. The query is immediately executed in the selected virtual warehouse. The query takes advantage of the computational resources assigned to the selected virtual warehouse. The available CPU, memory, and other resources that the query can employ are determined by the warehouse size.

Snowflake allows you to modify the size of the virtual warehouse while a query is in progress. Depending on your demands, you can upscale (raise its size) or downscale (reduce its size). Snowflake dynamically distributes fresh resources to the warehouse when the warehouse size is changed. When you scale up, the warehouse gets extra resources for query execution. It receives fewer resources when you downscale.

Here's the interesting part: despite the fact that the warehouse size has changed, the query continues to run in the same virtual warehouse where it began. It is not shifted or interrupted as a result of the size change. The query executes until it completes, using the resources available in the virtual warehouse at the time.

This method of query execution in Snowflake has several significant advantages. Query Consistency is maintained and queries are executed in the same warehouse-size cluster from start to finish, ensuring consistent performance characteristics. There are no outages or migrations to other clusters. Snowflake ensures that the query benefits from the new resource allocation when the warehouse size is changed during query execution. This offers greater flexibility in task management while avoiding query interruption.

Snowflake dynamically adjusts resources in response to workload demands. Query execution in the same warehouse-size cluster optimizes resource use and reduces overhead associated with query movement. Predictable Performance is also a factor. Users may expect consistent query performancc bccause the resources given to the query remain constant from start to finish, regardless of warehouse size changes.

Query Management is done by modifying warehouse sizes as needed. Organizations may simply manage and regulate query execution without affecting running queries. Scalability is a very important factor and if a query is executing in a warehouse and you expect it to require more resources to complete rapidly, you can increase the warehouse size to provide more resources. This is very beneficial for queries that require a lot of resources.

Cost Optimization is key here. If a query does not require a huge amount of resources, you can downscale a warehouse. This helps to keep cost under control because you are only paying for the resources that are required, especially for for mixed workloads. The option to modify the warehouse size during query execution is invaluable in systems with mixed workloads, where various queries have differing resource requirements. It ensures that each query obtains the resources it requires without interfering with others.

Handling Load Spikes is important. If there is an unexpected rise in query activity, you can upgrade warehouses to accommodate the extra demand, ensuring that all queries continue to execute without interruption.

Recommended practices to make the most of this Snowflake feature:

- **Keep an Eye on Query Performance**: Monitor query performance and resource consumption on a continuous basis to make informed decisions about when to upscale or downscale warehouses.
- **Resource Planning**: To reduce the need for frequent size changes, size your virtual warehouses suitably, depending on the predicted query workloads.
- **Query Optimization**: Invest in query optimization efforts to ensure that queries run efficiently and make the best use of the resources available.
- **Change Warehouse Sizes Strategically**: Change the warehouse size strategically during query execution, taking into account the query's resource requirements and overall workload.

Snowflake's unique query execution strategy, in which queries begin and conclude in the same warehouse-size cluster, provides constant performance, resource efficiency, and flexibility. This architecture enables you to modify warehouse sizes during query execution to match changing workload demands, allowing you to manage and improve query performance in Snowflake's cloud data warehousing environment in a smooth and efficient manner.

Warehouse Size

Snowflake offers a variety of virtual warehouse sizes to support a mix of workloads and query demands, ranging from X-Small to the most powerful 6X-Large. The quantity of processing resources allocated for query execution is determined by the size of a virtual warehouse. In this section, we'll look at the various warehouse sizes and underline how larger warehouses with more nodes have a substantial impact on the performance of larger and more complicated queries.

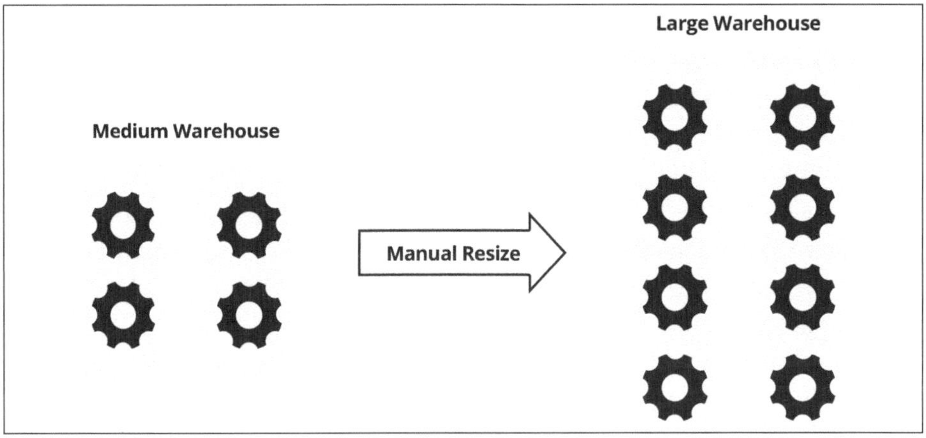

Figure 3.1: *Warehouse Size*

In the preceding figure, you can see how by increasing the size, you can make the warehouse twice as powerful with each increase in size.

Understanding the Warehouse Sizes of Snowflake

Snowflake provides a variety of virtual warehouse sizes, each optimized to certain use cases and workload needs.

Here's a rundown of the various warehouse sizes:

- **X-Small (XS):** This is the smallest virtual warehouse size, which is intended for modest workloads and small datasets. It uses fewer resources, yet is inexpensive for simple queries and data exploration.
- **Small (S):** The Small warehouse size is appropriate for light to medium workloads. It has more computational power than the X-Small, thus it's appropriate for scenarios with slightly larger datasets and moderately sophisticated queries.
- **Medium (M):** The Medium warehouse has significantly more computational resources than the Small warehouse. It is well-suited to medium-sized workloads, interactive data processing, and ad hoc queries.
- **Large (L):** The Large warehouse size is ideal for heavier workloads, complicated analytical queries, and larger datasets. It provides ample resources to perform intensive data processing operations.
- **X-Large (XL):** The X-Large warehouse is intended for high-performance workloads and enterprises with significant data processing needs, with

adequate computational resources for handling massive datasets and complicated queries.

- **2X-Large (2XL):** This warehouse-size has more resources than the X-Large, making it appropriate for data-intensive applications, advanced analytics, and scenarios demanding high query concurrency.
- **3X-Large (3XL):** The 3X-Large warehouse size is excellent for enterprises that require a large amount of data analytics. It significantly increases resource availability, allowing for faster query execution and scalability.
- **4X-Large (4XL):** This warehouse size is intended for large-scale data processing and advanced analytics. It has a large amount of computational capability to handle sophisticated queries and large workloads.
- **5X-Large (5XL):** The 5X-Large warehouse size is ideal for enterprises with high data analytics demands. It has plenty of resources to process massive datasets, conduct complicated queries, and achieve high concurrency.
- **6X-Large (6XL):** The 6X-Large virtual warehouse is the most powerful, with the biggest computational resources. It is well-suited to data-intensive applications such as real-time analytics and large-scale data conversions.

Larger warehouse sizes like X-Large, 2X-Large, 3X-Large, 4X-Large, 5X-Large, and 6X-Large have a significant influence on query performance, especially for larger and more sophisticated queries. They make a difference in the following ways:

- **Increased Computational Power**: Because larger warehouses have more nodes, they have more CPU and memory resources available for query execution. This increased computational capability allows them to do more complex calculations and transformations more quickly.
- **Parallelism**: Larger warehouses can conduct queries over several nodes in parallel. Because of this parallelism, they can divide query jobs into smaller subtasks and process them concurrently. As a result, complex searches can be handled more quickly.
- **Memory Capacity**: Larger warehouses have more memory, which is advantageous for caching intermediate results and temporary data during query execution. This lowers the need to access slower storage tiers, such as object storage or data lakes, resulting in faster query performance.
- **Concurrency**: Larger warehouses can handle more queries concurrently. They can handle several queries running concurrently without resource contention, making them appropriate for heavy query burden scenarios.

When you designate a larger warehouse to a query, Snowflake ensures that the query receives a larger share of available resources. This optimized resource allocation improves query performance even further. Data Processing Intensity, for queries that need resource-intensive procedures, such as complicated aggregations, transformations, or joins on huge datasets, benefits greatly from larger warehouses' compute power and memory capacity.

Choosing the correct warehouse size is critical for obtaining optimal query performance and cost efficiency. Consider the following factors when selecting the appropriate size:

- **Workload Evaluation**: Examine your workload patterns, paying special attention to query complexity, dataset size, and concurrency requirements. Different warehouse sizes may help different workloads.
- **Query Optimization**: Make an investment in query optimization to guarantee that your queries are as efficient as possible. Queries that are well-optimized can perform effectively even with smaller warehouse sizes.
- **Scaling Resources**: Be prepared to scale your warehouse size up or down depending on workload demands. The flexibility of Snowflake to dynamically modify warehouse size enables cost-effective resource allocation.
- **Cost Control**: Larger warehouse sizes have higher costs. Balance performance requirements with economic considerations to ensure that resources are used efficiently.
- **Concurrency Requirements**: Think about how many concurrent queries your company needs to support. Larger warehouses are better suited to high-traffic regions.
- **Data Expansion**: Plan for data expansion over time. As your dataset grows, you may need to increase the capacity of your warehouse to maintain performance.

Consider the following best practices to make the most of increased warehouse sizes:

- **Keep an Eye on Resource Usage**: Monitor resource utilization in your warehouse on a regular basis to verify that you are maximizing the available processing power.
- **Query Optimization**: Constantly improve your queries to make the best use of the resources offered by larger warehouses.
- **Scaling Resources**: Be prepared to scale your warehouse size in response to fluctuations in query demand. Costs can be reduced by scaling up during peak periods and down during off-peak periods.

- **Concurrency Management**: Utilize query prioritization and workload management tools to efficiently distribute resources, particularly in high-concurrency scenarios.

Experiment with different warehouse sizes to find the best balance of performance and cost for your individual workloads.

Snowflake's virtual warehouses come in a variety of sizes, each designed to meet the needs of a specific workload. Larger warehouse sizes have a substantial influence on the performance of larger and more complicated queries due to more nodes and computational resources. However, choosing the proper warehouse size based on your workload characteristics is critical, as is continuously optimizing queries and being prepared to modify warehouse sizes dynamically to achieve the best combination of query performance and cost efficiency.

Warehouse Clusters

The cloud data warehousing technology from Snowflake is primarily reliant on warehouse concurrency. It refers to the ability of a Snowflake virtual warehouse to handle multiple queries at once. By successfully controlling warehouse concurrency, organizations can improve query performance, increase resource efficiency, and provide a responsive analytics environment. We'll discuss warehouse concurrency, why it's important, and how adding more clusters increases the number of concurrent queries running on the system.

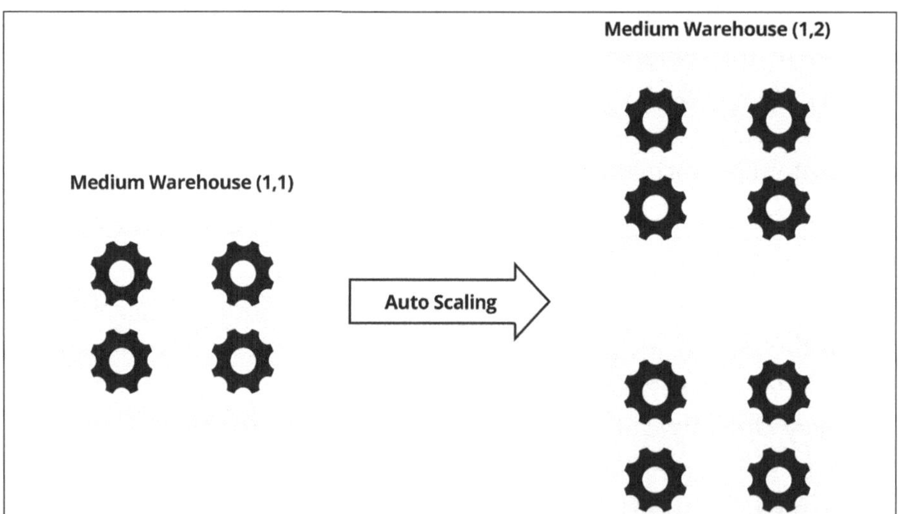

Figure 3.2: *Warehouse Auto Scale*

In the preceding figure, you can see how you can increase concurrency by adding more clusters it might have the same nodes as a large warehouse but in just two medium warehouses

Warehouse concurrency refers to a Snowflake virtual warehouse's capacity to run many queries concurrently. It's an important consideration when designing a data analytics architecture because it has a direct impact on the system's ability to handle user requests efficiently. Snowflake's concurrency control solution is unique and successful. Rather than setting a fixed amount of concurrent queries, Snowflake uses a dynamic, adaptive technique to limit concurrency. It allows users to specify the maximum number of queries that can run concurrently within a virtual warehouse using the "*Warehouse Max Concurrency*" parameter. Snowflake, on the other hand, intelligently handles concurrency, prioritizing key queries and optimizing resource allocation.

Warehouse concurrency is critical and has a number of significant implications for Snowflake-using organizations:

- **Responsive User Experience**: Concurrency management guarantees that customers wait as little as possible for query replies, resulting in a more responsive and user-friendly analytics environment.
- **Consumption of Resources**: Concurrency that is properly managed maximizes the usage of computing resources within a virtual warehouse, such as CPU and memory. This ensures that resources are distributed efficiently and are not squandered on idle or low-priority requests.
- **Query Performance**: Effective concurrency management enables high-priority queries to swiftly obtain the resources they demand, leading to improved query performance. Users can run complex queries with no resource limitations.
- **Scalability**: Snowflake's ability to dynamically distribute resources depending on concurrent requirements ensures that the system can scale efficiently to meet rising demand.

Cost control is aided by effective concurrency management, which ensures that resources are allocated just as needed, preventing over-provisioning. Concurrency can be increased by adding more clusters.

Snowflake's concurrency can be boosted by adding more clusters or virtual warehouses to your environment. Increasing the number of clusters has the following effect on concurrency:

- **Cluster Parallelism**: Each virtual warehouse operates independently, with its own set of computational resources. By adding more virtual warehouses (clusters), you can increase the overall processing capacity available for query execution.

- **Resource Isolation**: Using many clusters enhances resource isolation. Queries in one virtual warehouse do not interfere with queries in another. This isolation is especially important in situations where query priority changes.
- **Concurrent Query Handling**: As the number of clusters increases, so does the system's ability to handle concurrent queries. Up to the Warehouse Max Concurrency setting, each virtual warehouse can run queries in parallel.
- **Concurrency Scaling**: As the number of clusters increases, Snowflake's ability to dynamically scale resources up or down based on workload requirements improves. It ensures that resources are dispersed optimally, even during peak query periods.

One of the most important questions in concurrency is when should we add more clusters.

There are several practical cases when adding more clusters is advantageous:

- **Large Query Workloads**: Adding many clusters to maintain responsive query performance may benefit enterprises with high query volumes or demanding workloads such as real-time analytics or ad hoc querying.
- **Workload Variation**: To improve concurrency in systems with a mix of query kinds, such as brief, interactive searches and long-running, complex queries, different clusters might be given to each query type.

When it comes to query prioritization, using dedicated clusters for high-priority requests ensures that they receive immediate attention and resources. Balancing and distributing query workloads over multiple clusters helps to distribute compute loads, reduce resource bottlenecks, and maintain equal resource allocation.

Consider the following best practices for efficiently managing warehouse concurrency:

- **Monitoring**: Workloads should be monitored in real-time to better understand resource use, query complexity, and performance patterns.
- **Warehouse Sizing**: Choose the appropriate virtual warehouse sizes for your use cases, keeping in mind the expected concurrency requirements.
- **Warehouse Scaling**: Be ready to scale virtual warehouses up or down in response to workload fluctuations. Snowflake's ability to dynamically adjust warehouse sizes is an excellent resource management tool.

Use query prioritization methods to ensure that high-priority requests receive adequate resources, especially during peak periods of high concurrency. Configure virtual warehouses and clusters to precisely match the needs of your workloads. Assign various clusters to different query types or departments to maximize resource use. Set acceptable Warehouse Max Concurrency limits depending on each virtual warehouse's estimated usage. Consider the implications for performance as well as cost.

Let us examine a few scenarios where the auto-scaling and caching capabilities of Snowflake warehouses can be crucial. For instance, a retail organization may have substantial surges in data processing requirements during holiday seasons or during special campaigns.

Snowflake's elastic scaling enables the organization to effortlessly include extra computational resources to manage the surge in demand, guaranteeing optimal performance during periods of high activity. This facilitates the efficient management of heightened workloads without impacting routine operations. The marketing team is required to assess the efficacy of different campaigns by analyzing extensive datasets that encompass user interactions and engagement metrics. The marketing team is able to efficiently process and analyze huge amounts of data because of Snowflake's capacity to automatically adjust its scalability according to the workload. They can utilize features such as auto-suspension to optimize expenses during periods of system inactivity.

Query performance may be hindered by frequently accessible datasets in some organizations and the result set caching feature of Snowflake enables the system to save and reuse the outcomes of frequently conducted queries. This minimizes the necessity of repeatedly reprocessing the same data, enhancing the overall performance of queries and reducing resource use. Please note that the use of examples provided are general in nature, and the actual implementation may differ depending on the individual needs and settings of each organization.

The data warehousing capabilities of Snowflake rely largely on warehouse concurrency. It describes the system's ability to handle multiple requests at once, which influences user experience, resource utilization, and overall query performance. Adding more clusters to your Snowflake system improves concurrency by enabling simultaneous query execution across virtual warehouses. This scalability ensures that the system can handle increased workloads while maintaining optimal query performance. For companies wishing to reap the benefits of Snowflake's cloud data warehousing technology, effective warehouse concurrency management is key.

Warehouse Scaling Policy

The Warehouse Scaling Policies, which include the Economy and Standard policies, are critical components of Snowflake's cloud data warehousing platform. By automatically altering the number of clusters of virtual warehouses based on workload demands, these policies enable enterprises to achieve a balance between cost efficiency and query performance. In this section, we will look into Snowflake's Warehouse Scaling policies, explain how the Economy and Standard policies function, and describe how enterprises can benefit from them.

Snowflake provides two Warehouse Scaling Policies to dynamically manage the resources assigned to virtual warehouses. These policies manage clusters on the virtual warehouses automatically based on query concurrency and resource use, ensuring optimal performance and cost-efficiency.

The Economy Scaling Policy is intended to prioritize cost savings while maintaining acceptable query performance. It tries to save money by starting with a small virtual warehouse and gradually expanding its cluster count as query concurrency and resource utilization increase. This policy is appropriate for workloads where cost conservation is a top priority.

The Standard Scaling Policy strikes a compromise between cost efficiency and query performance. By starting with a fairly sized virtual warehouse and altering its cluster count based on query concurrency and resource use, it seeks to deliver a responsive and optimal query environment. The Standard Policy is suited for general-purpose workloads that require cost control as well as query efficiency.

The Economy and Standard Scaling Policies function similarly, automatically altering the clusters of a virtual warehouse depending on particular criteria. When you create a virtual warehouse, you specify the size and cluster min and max values. This cluster min value sets the warehouse's initial computational resources.

The Economy and Standard policies analyze the workload when query concurrency increases, suggesting a higher need for resources. The policies initiate an automatic addition of the new clusters in the event that the concurrency level is achieved or exceeded. When a virtual warehouse gets more clusters, it is dynamically scaled up to a greater size with more processing resources (for example, CPU and memory). This ensures that the warehouse can adequately handle the additional query workload.

Cost-effectiveness is ensured by controls that continuously monitor resource consumption and query concurrency. When the workload and concurrency fall below a specific level, the virtual warehouse clusters are reduced making it more cost-effective. The virtual warehouse's dynamic scaling guarantees that query performance stays optimal, with the capacity to scale resources up during high demand and down during periods of low activity.

For enterprises seeking cost-effective and performance-optimized data analytics environments, leveraging Snowflake's Economy and Standard Scaling Policies can provide considerable benefits.

The Economy Policy is suitable for enterprises that want to keep cloud costs predictable and under control. It starts with few resources and scales up only as necessary, avoiding over-provisioning. Organizations can optimize cloud spending while maintaining reasonable query performance by selecting the Economy Policy, making it suited for scenarios with tight budget limits.

Organizations can utilize the Economy Policy for development and testing environments to reduce costs during periods of low activity.

The Standard Policy provides a balanced approach by guaranteeing that virtual warehouses are large enough to handle common query workloads efficiently. Organizations may rely on the Standard Policy to automatically scale resources during peak hours, ensuring that query performance stays consistent. Standard Policy is suitable for a wide range of workloads. It is a versatile alternative for enterprises with varying query requirements.

Both approaches adjust to shifting demand patterns, allowing businesses to handle varied levels of query concurrency without manual intervention. Users need to monitor query concurrency and resources used to fine-tune scaling policies in response to changing workload patterns. Resource efficiency is ensured by the policies, with virtual warehouses scaling up to meet demand and scaling down during idle periods. Organizations may keep query performance high while using resources wisely, resulting in a cost-effective and responsive analytics environment.

Automating the resizing of virtual warehouses eliminates the need for manual intervention, reducing administrative work and guaranteeing that resources are always optimum. Organizations may handle increased query workloads without the difficulties of manual resource allocation, making data analytics processes easier to scale.

Economy and Standard Scaling Policies are suitable for a wide range of use cases and industries. The Economy Policy can help organizations manage cloud expenses effectively while maintaining adequate query performance. Industries that require general-purpose data analytics, such as e-commerce, banking, or healthcare, can rely on the Standard Policy for a cost-performance balance.

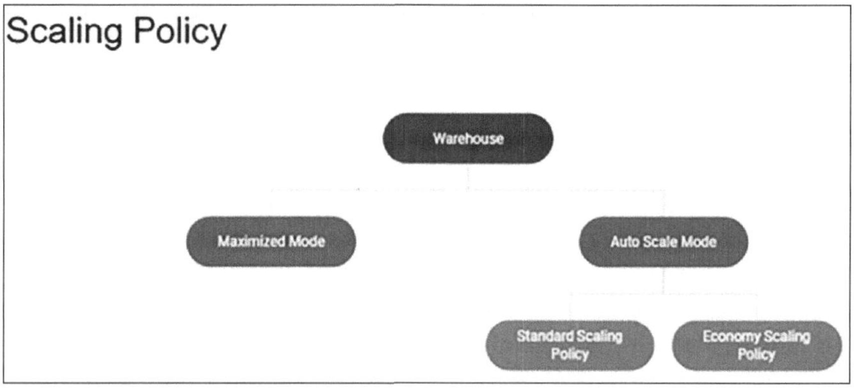

***Figure 3.3**: SnowFlake Scaling Policy*

In the preceding figure, you can see the various options in the warehouse mode and scaling policy.

Development and testing environments, where resource needs fluctuate, can use the Economy Policy during non-working hours to reduce expenditures. Retail and Seasonal enterprises can get the best of both approaches and can be used with seasonal demand to meet fluctuating enquiry patterns and expense restrictions.

Consider the following best practices to make the most of Snowflake's Economy and Standard Scaling Policies:

- **Workload Analysis**: Examine your query workload trends to identify which scaling policy best corresponds with the aims of your organization. Select appropriate initial virtual warehouse sizes depending on predicted query concurrency and resource requirements.
- **Continuous Monitoring**: Monitor query concurrency and resource use on a regular basis to verify that policies are in sync with changing workload patterns.
- **Scheduled Maintenance**: Schedule maintenance work during periods of low activity to reduce costs, particularly when adopting the Economy Policy.
- **Query Optimization**: Invest in query optimization efforts to guarantee that queries, regardless of warehouse size, are as efficient as feasible.

Experiment with both strategies to see which one achieves the best mix of cost and performance for your specific workloads. Snowflake's Economy and

Standard Scaling Policies are useful tools for businesses looking to improve cost-efficiency and query performance in their data analytics setups. These policies provide a balanced approach to cost control and performance improvement by automatically altering the size of virtual warehouses based on query concurrency and resource use. To guarantee that their data analytics operations are efficient, cost-effective, and responsive to changing demands, organizations can choose the policy that best corresponds with their goals and use cases, fine-tune resource sizing, and regularly analyze workload patterns.

Warehouse Auto Suspend and Resume

The **Auto Suspend** and **Auto Resume** features in Snowflake are effective solutions for improving cost-efficiency and resource management in cloud data warehousing. These features allow businesses to pause (suspend) and resume virtual warehouses based on user-defined criteria, ensuring that computational resources are only active when needed. In this section, we'll go through Snowflake's Auto Suspend and Auto Resume capabilities, describing how they function and how businesses can use them to their advantage.

Snowflake's Auto Suspend feature allows customers to automatically stop or suspend a virtual warehouse after a specified time of inactivity. When a virtual warehouse is suspended, all of its computational resources, including CPU and memory, are released, and the warehouse enters a sleep state. This feature is especially valuable for lowering cloud computing expenses by preventing resources from being consumed while they are not in use.

Auto Resume is the opposite of Auto Suspend. It enables users to set the criteria under which a suspended virtual warehouse will resume or wake up automatically. When a virtual warehouse is restarted, it becomes operational once more, and users can begin executing queries without the need for manual intervention. Auto Resume guarantees that the virtual warehouse is always available and ready for use, decreasing user wait times.

Auto Suspend and Auto Resume are simple to set up and utilize in Snowflake and users can configure the Auto Suspend time, which denotes the amount of inactivity (in minutes) after which the virtual warehouse will automatically suspend. This period can be modified based on the workload trends of the organization. Snowflake monitors user activity and query execution within the virtual warehouse in real-time. If no action occurs during the chosen Auto Suspend time, the virtual warehouse will suspend itself. When the virtual warehouse is suspended, all allocated resources are released, and the cost of the virtual warehouse stops accruing. This guarantees that resources are used efficiently, especially during periods of low or no activity.

Users can configure the Auto Resume condition, which describes the requirements that must be met for the virtual warehouse to resume automatically. Time-based schedules, scheduled tasks, and external occurrences are examples of conditions. Snowflake checks whether the Auto Resume conditions are met on a regular basis. This validation ensures that the virtual warehouse is suspended until the conditions provided are met. Snowflake automatically resumes the virtual warehouse when the Auto Resume conditions are met. The warehouse becomes operational and ready to process requests.

Using Snowflake's Auto Suspend and Auto Resume functionality gives enterprises various benefits. Auto Suspend assists enterprises in lowering cloud expenses by ensuring that resources are only activated when they are required. This eliminates excessive charges from accruing during downtime. Auto Suspend also facilitates optimal use of computing resources by releasing resources during inactivity, allowing other virtual warehouses to benefit from available resources. Auto Resume reduces the need for manual intervention to reactivate a suspended virtual warehouse. This saves administrative costs while also ensuring that resources are available when needed by users.

Organizations can tailor Auto Resume conditions to their individual workload patterns and business requirements. This adaptability ensures that virtual warehouses are always available when needed. Organizations can plan for consistent query performance with Auto Resume, knowing that virtual warehouses will automatically activate when demand increases. Auto Resume enables automated scaling depending on user-defined parameters, allowing virtual warehouses to adapt to shifting workloads without requiring manual adjustments.

Snowflake's Auto Suspend and Auto Resume functions are useful in a variety of situations:

- **Intermittent Workloads**: Auto Suspend and Auto Resume can help organizations with workloads that have irregular activity patterns, such as batch processing or scheduled reporting, by ensuring resource availability during active periods. Development and testing of virtual warehouses can be designed to automatically suspend during non-working hours, lowering expenses while ensuring availability during the daytime.
- **Scheduled ETL Operations**: Organizations operating ETL pipelines (Extract, Transform, Load) can use Auto Resume to ensure that virtual

warehouses are active when scheduled ETL operations need to be performed, ensuring timely data processing.

- **Ad Hoc Analytics**: Ad hoc data analysis teams can benefit from Auto Suspend to decrease expenses during inactivity, while Auto Resume guarantees resources are accessible for spontaneous analysis. Organizations wishing to limit cloud expenses can utilize Auto Suspend to proactively monitor resource utilization, minimizing unexpected pricing increases.
- **Scaling with Demand**: Auto Resume can be configured to automatically scale virtual warehouses during peak usage hours, maintaining consistent query performance without the need for manual intervention.

Consider the following best practices while using Snowflake's Auto Suspend and Auto Resume features:

- **Workload Evaluation**: Analyze your workload patterns to discover the best Auto Suspend and Auto Resume settings for your organization's needs. Adjusting the size of your virtual warehouses to match the workload requirements can have an influence on the cost reductions gained by Auto Suspend.
- **Schedule Optimization**: Align Auto Resume criteria with your organization's working hours to ensure virtual warehouses are active when users are actively searching data. Monitoring and alerting methods should be implemented to keep track of virtual warehouse suspensions, resumptions, and resource use.
- **Query prioritizing**: When a virtual warehouse resumes, employ query prioritizing capabilities to guarantee that high-priority queries receive resources as soon as possible. Regularly evaluate your Auto Suspend and Auto Resume options to ensure they are still in sync with your changing workload patterns and business requirements.

Snowflake's Auto Suspend and Auto Resume functionalities are critical for improving cost-efficiency and resource management in cloud data warehousing. Auto Suspend allows enterprises to halt virtual warehouses automatically during periods of inactivity, while Auto Resume guarantees that resources are available when needed. Taking advantage of these characteristics results in cost savings, more efficient resource utilization, and a more responsive analytics environment, all while decreasing the need for manual intervention. Organizations can utilize the full potential of Snowflake's cloud data warehousing platform while efficiently limiting cloud expenses by carefully selecting and modifying Auto Suspend and Auto Resume settings to match workload patterns and business demands.

Warehouse Query Timeout

The query timeout feature in Snowflake is an important tool for regulating query execution and preventing runaway queries from consuming excessive computing resources or significantly impacting the performance of your data warehouse. Users can select a limited duration for a query to perform using this feature. If the query's timeout period is exceeded, Snowflake will immediately end it. In this section, we will look at how Snowflake's query timeout works and how it may be used to stop runaway queries.

Query timeout is a function in Snowflake for limiting the execution time of SQL queries. It's especially useful for avoiding queries that find unanticipated difficulties or inefficiencies from running forever, which could result in resource contention and poor performance.

Setting the Timeout can be done at different levels, like user session and warehouse, and when submitting a query, users can select a query timeout value. This value represents the maximum amount of time (in seconds) that the query can run. When a query is executed, Snowflake records the amount of time that has passed. If the query is finished within the set timeout, the results are returned normally. If the query execution time exceeds the timeout value, Snowflake will terminate the query automatically. The query is terminated by force, and any partial results are discarded.

Query timeout in a warehouse prevents queries that are stalled or inefficient from using up too many processing resources. This ensures that other queries and workloads can continue to operate without interruption. Snowflake helps maintain consistent query speed by terminating long-running queries, ensuring that users obtain results quickly, even in multi-tenant setups. By reducing wasteful resource utilization, runaway queries can help control cloud computing costs. When a query times out, users receive timely feedback, which may lead them to refine their queries or consider alternate ways, thereby improving the overall user experience.

Query timeout is useful in a variety of situations, like exploring data ad hoc, users may unwittingly submit queries with unwanted implications. A query timeout can keep these inquiries from interfering with other users or the system. Queries using complex joins, aggregations, or big datasets may take longer than expected on occasion. The query timeout ensures that such requests do not monopolize resources indefinitely. Query timeout can catch queries that become inefficient due to code changes in development and testing settings where queries are iteratively adjusted.

Query timeout also helps preserve fairness in multi-tenant systems where several users or departments share resources by preventing individual requests from monopolizing resources.

To make the most of Snowflake's query timeout feature, define query timeout values that correspond to the average query execution time in your environment. Set timeouts carefully, as doing so, may result in the premature termination of legitimate inquiries and also keep an eye on query performance and execution timings regularly. Adjust query timeouts as appropriate in response to changing workload patterns.

Encourage query optimization efforts to reduce the likelihood of queries exceeding the timeout threshold. Queries that are efficient are less likely to be terminated prematurely. Educate users on the purpose of the query timeout functionality. Encourage them to optimize their queries and gracefully handle timeouts. Implement logging and monitoring techniques to track queries that frequently exceed the timeout threshold. Utilize this information for query optimization and debugging.

The query timeout function in Snowflake is an important tool for regulating query execution and preventing runaway queries, which can have a detrimental influence on system performance and resource use. Organizations can ensure that queries are completed in a reasonable timeframe and that computing resources are utilized efficiently by defining a maximum permissible execution time for queries. Query timeout aids in the preservation of cost control, query performance, and a timely data analytics environment, hence improving the overall user experience. Setting realistic timeouts, monitoring query performance, encouraging query optimization, educating users, and establishing logging and monitoring systems to track and manage queries effectively all contribute to effective query timeout utilization.

Warehouse Maximized Mode

The Snowflake cloud data warehousing platform's Warehouse Maximized Mode is a customized resource allocation configuration. It is intended for certain use scenarios in which maximizing performance, typically at the price of cost, is the primary goal. In this section, we'll look at what Warehouse Maximized Mode is, how it works, and which use cases are most suited to this resource allocation setting.

The Warehouse Maximized Mode in Snowflake allows businesses to aggressively allocate computational resources to a virtual warehouse, basically offering it priority access to available resources. Warehouse Maximized Mode favors performance over other resource allocation modes, which aim for a balance of performance and cost. As a result, it is frequently more resource-intensive and more expensive.

When a virtual warehouse is set to function in Warehouse Maximized Mode, it obtains higher resource priority when compared to other warehouses in the same account, the virtual warehouse receives a much bigger share of available computational resources. CPU, memory, and I/O resources are all included. The virtual warehouse in Warehouse Maximized Mode may accommodate more concurrent queries. This makes it appropriate for applications with high-concurrency requirements. The virtual warehouse's resources remain relatively steady and are less likely to be dynamically transferred to other warehouses, maintaining consistent performance. Due to the significant resource allocation, running a virtual warehouse in Warehouse Maximized Mode may be more expensive than other allocation options.

Warehouse Maximized Mode is ideally suited for specific use situations in which optimizing query performance is more important than cost considerations. Organizations that require real-time or near-real-time analytics processing. Because of the improved resources and concurrency, queries may be executed quickly, providing immediate insights. Workloads involving complicated analytical queries, such as advanced data modeling, machine learning, or data transformation, might benefit from significant resource allocation to execute these activities quickly and efficiently. In scenarios involving huge datasets or large-scale data processing operations, Warehouse Maximized Mode can ensure that queries are completed as quickly as possible, decreasing the time required to draw insights.

Organizations that rely on live, interactive dashboards for essential decision-making processes can employ Warehouse Maximized Mode to ensure consistent, high-performance access to these dashboards, even during peak demand periods. In environments where multiple users are conducting ad hoc queries concurrently, such as during data exploration or discovery phases, Warehouse Maximized Mode can be used to ensure that all users have responsive query performance.

Warehouse Maximized Mode has its own benefits. Applications can get better query performance because of its high resource allocation. Warehouse Maximized Mode provides great query performance, ensuring that queries are performed promptly and effectively. The mode is well-suited for managing a large number of concurrent queries, making it appropriate for use cases requiring high concurrency. The virtual warehouse's resources stay stable, limiting the impact of resource contention or fluctuations on query performance. Organizations can gain timely insights and make data-driven decisions more quickly, especially in scenarios requiring real-time or near-real-time analytics.

While Warehouse Maximized Mode provides considerable performance gains, there are a few things to keep in mind:

- **Cost:** Due to the significant resource allotment, running a virtual warehouse in Warehouse Maximized Mode might be costly. Organizations should carefully consider the costs and budget accordingly.
- **Resource Allocation:** Keep in mind that this mode utilizes a larger portion of available resources, which may have an impact on the performance of other concurrent workloads in the same account.
- **Workload Type:** This mode is best suited for workloads that demand peak performance and can justify the related expense. It may not be the most cost-effective option for all applications.
- **Monitoring and Optimization:** To optimize the use of Warehouse Maximized Mode, organizations should regularly monitor resource use and query performance.

The Warehouse Maximized Mode in Snowflake is a resource allocation mode designed for situations where extraordinary query performance takes precedence over cost considerations. It provides significant performance, concurrency handling, and timely insights, making it perfect for real-time analytics, complicated analytical workloads, large-scale data processing, interactive dashboards, and high-concurrency ad hoc queries. However, before choosing Warehouse Maximized Mode, organizations should carefully consider the cost implications and resource requirements, as it might be more expensive than other allocation options.

Warehouse Max Concurrency Level

The Warehouse Max Concurrency Level in Snowflake's cloud data warehousing technology limits the number of queries a virtual warehouse can handle concurrently. It is a critical metric for improving query performance and resource utilization. It is crucial to note, however, that the Warehouse Max Concurrency Level should not be interpreted as a rigid top limit for concurrency. In this detailed section, we'll look at what the Warehouse Max Concurrency Level is, why it's important, and why it should be considered as a tool rather than an absolute requirement.

The Warehouse Max Concurrency Level is a setting that specifies the maximum number of concurrent queries that a virtual warehouse can run. Virtual warehouses are computing resources in Snowflake that are used for query execution. They can be dynamically scaled to handle changing workloads and query needs. The Warehouse Max Concurrency Level manages resource allocation within a virtual warehouse, ensuring that queries run efficiently and without resource contention. The Warehouse Max Concurrency Level fulfills numerous critical functions. It governs how computational resources, like as CPU, memory, and storage, are assigned to concurrent queries within a virtual warehouse. This allotment is critical for query performance and response. Organizations can improve query performance by configuring an appropriate Warehouse Max Concurrency Level. This guarantees that queries run efficiently and without bottlenecks, resulting in faster results and a better user experience.

Managing concurrency is crucial for controlling cloud computing expenses. Organizations can combine query performance with cost-efficiency by choosing an ideal Warehouse Max Concurrency Level, ensuring they only employ the resources they require. The Warehouse Max Concurrency Level aids in preventing resource contention among queries. Isolating workloads ensures that the resource utilization of one query does not significantly impact the performance of another.

It is critical to understand that the Warehouse Max Concurrency Level should not be regarded as a hard upper limit for concurrency. It is instead a dynamic parameter that can be changed to accommodate varying workloads and query demands. Snowflake's virtual warehouses are built to scale dynamically. Organizations can scale them up or down as needed to allocate more or fewer resources. That is, even though the Warehouse Max Concurrency Level is initially set to a fixed number, it can be modified in real-time to match changing workload requirements.

The real concurrency that a virtual warehouse can handle is determined by the availability of processing resources. A virtual warehouse with more resources (for example, a larger size) may accommodate a higher level of concurrency. Reduced accessible resources, on the other hand, may reduce effective concurrency.

Not all queries need the same level of computational resources. Simple searches can run quickly and use fewer resources, allowing for more concurrency. Complex queries or resource-intensive activities may necessitate more resources, lowering the possible concurrency. Snowflake allows organizations to prioritize queries based on their importance or urgency. Organizations can successfully control concurrency, even when resources are limited by distributing resources selectively to high-priority queries.

The Warehouse Max Concurrency Level should be seen as a malleable parameter that businesses can tailor to their own requirements. Constantly monitor query workloads to gain insight into resource use, query complexity, and performance. This information can be used to make judgments about adjusting the Warehouse Max Concurrency Level. Prepare to scale up or down virtual warehouses based on workload demands. Increasing the available resources can handle more concurrency, whilst decreasing resources can assist to control expenses during low-demand periods.

Implement query prioritization algorithms to ensure that important or time-sensitive queries receive appropriate resources even when concurrency is high. This helps to keep key operations responsive.

Make an investment in query optimization to reduce resource consumption and query execution times. Queries that are well-optimized can withstand greater concurrent levels without decreasing performance. Try different Warehouse Max Concurrency Level settings to discover the best blend of performance and cost-efficiency for your individual workloads.

The Warehouse Max Concurrency Level must be adjusted to accommodate different use cases and workload patterns during busy periods, such as month-end financial reporting or holiday sales, businesses may need to increase the Warehouse Max Concurrency Level to guarantee query execution is timely and performance SLAs are met. Workloads involving ad hoc queries, in which users investigate data interactively, benefit from flexibility in concurrency control. Based on user activities, the Warehouse Max Concurrency Level can be changed.

When executing batch procedures that entail resource-intensive data transformations or ETL (Extract, Transform, Load) operations, organizations may temporarily lower the Warehouse Max Concurrency Level to allocate extra resources to each query and by monitoring query performance and resource utilization on a regular basis, businesses can make real-time changes to the Warehouse Max Concurrency Level. This guarantees that resource allocation corresponds to query requirements.

Analyze your workload patterns on a regular basis to understand resource requirements and concurrency requirements and be ready to scale virtual warehouses up or down based on workload demands.

Implement query priority algorithms to guarantee that key queries receive the resources they require and put efforts into query optimization to reduce resource usage and enhance query efficiency.

Experiment with different Warehouse Max Concurrency Level settings to discover the best blend of performance and cost-efficiency.

The Warehouse Max Concurrency Level in Snowflake is a dynamic option that is critical in managing query performance, resource allocation, and cost control inside virtual warehouses. While it specifies the maximum number of concurrent queries that a virtual warehouse can process, it should not be regarded as an absolute maximum. Instead, it should be viewed as a versatile instrument that businesses may use to adapt to changing workload demands and resource availability by properly managing the Warehouse.

Query Acceleration Service

Query Acceleration Service (QAS) is a strong feature meant to improve query performance while also optimizing cost-efficiency within the Snowflake cloud data warehousing platform. It employs cutting-edge indexing and caching techniques to significantly accelerate query execution, minimize data processing costs, and improve overall user experience. In this section, we'll go into the Query Acceleration Service, examine its essential components and benefits, and show how it can result in significant cost savings.

Snowflake automatically arranges data within tables into micro-partitions, enhancing data storage and retrieval. This procedure improves query performance by minimizing the quantity of data that must be scanned during query execution. Materialized views are precomputed, condensed views of data that can considerably improve query performance. Snowflake automatically discovers opportunities for materialized views based on query patterns and uses and creates them to expedite frequently executed queries.

By limiting data scanning and optimizing query strategies, the Query Acceleration Service significantly reduces query execution times. This results in faster response times for analytical and reporting queries. QAS enables queries to execute faster and that correlates to lower computational costs. Organizations can save significantly on cloud computing prices, especially in situations with massive datasets and complicated queries. With accelerated queries, enterprises can confidently meet performance SLAs and ensure a consistent user experience, even during peak workloads.

Snowflake's automatic clustering and materialized view construction reduce the need for human query tuning. Data engineers and analysts can concentrate on analysis and insights rather than query fine-tuning. Accelerated queries free up compute resources more quickly, allowing for higher query concurrency within the same computational footprint. This ensures that several users or programs can access and evaluate data at the same time without performance bottlenecks.

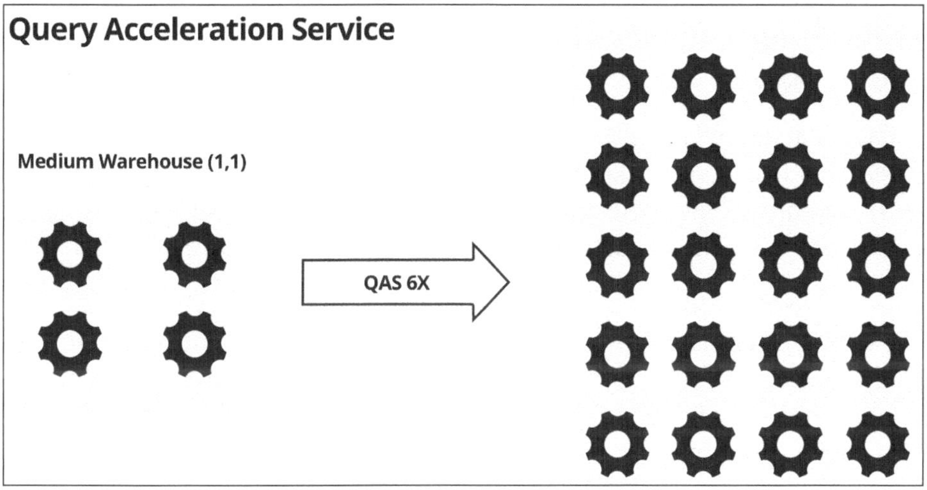

Figure 3.4: *Query Acceleration Service*

In the preceding figure, you can see how a medium warehouse can scale up to 6 times the size when we use QAS with a scale factor

Snowflake's Query Acceleration Service directly leads to cost savings, Accelerated queries complete faster, and they employ fewer computing resources. This means that enterprises will pay less for cloud computing services, resulting in immediate cost savings. Automatic clustering reduces storage costs by efficiently grouping data into micro-partitions. This not only improves query efficiency, but also minimizes the amount of data that must be stored in the cloud. Faster searches result in fewer data movement between storage and compute layers, resulting in cheaper data transfer costs within the cloud environment.

When queries perform more effectively, there is less need to scale up or out by adding additional virtual warehouses or clusters. This minimizes the amount of scaling events and associated costs.

Snowflake's per-second charging mechanism ensures that faster searches result in cheaper query charges. Organizations only pay for the time the query actually runs, not the time spent scanning data.

Query Acceleration Service can help a retail organization with a huge dataset to conduct complex analytical queries to acquire insights into customer behavior and inventory management. These queries are expedited by using Snowflake's Query Acceleration Service, which reduces the time and processing resources required. The corporation reduces its cloud computing expenses, resulting in significant cost savings. Financial institutions depend on Snowflake for financial reporting and regulatory compliance. Complex financial inquiries are completed much faster with the QAS. This not only provides timely reporting but also saves the firm on monthly cloud infrastructure costs.

Snowflake is used by a healthcare provider to analyze patient data and optimize healthcare delivery. The expedited searches improve the pace of data-driven decision-making. This efficiency results in a reduction in cloud computing expenses, allowing the organization to spend resources more strategically.

QAS can be used to maximize cost savings and this can be done by monitoring and optimizing queries on a regular basis. Snowflake's query profiling tools can help you identify performance bottlenecks and increase query efficiency. Investigate how materialized views can speed up your most frequently executed queries. Analyze query patterns and use them to determine which materialized views can have the most influence on query performance.

When importing data into Snowflake, use the automated clustering option. Load data into the proper tables and use clustering keys to guarantee the best data organization. Consider the size and quantity of virtual warehouses based on your workloads. Oversized warehouses can incur extra costs, while undersized warehouses might cause performance concerns.

Snowflake's query caching can enhance query performance and eliminate the need for repetitive data scans. Configure caching settings to meet your individual workload patterns.

Snowflake's QAS is a game changer for enterprises looking to improve query performance while saving money in their cloud data warehousing settings. Snowflake not only accelerates query execution but also decreases computing, storage, and data transmission costs by automating data clustering, materialized view building, and query optimization. These cost savings, combined with better query performance and concurrency, make Snowflake's Query Acceleration Service a great tool for enterprises aiming to optimize the value of their data analytics investments.

Snowpark Optimized Warehouses

Snowpark Optimized Warehouse is a resource allocation option that provides users with enhanced compute resources specifically intended for difficult data processing tasks such as machine learning and artificial intelligence (ML and AI). This mode is designed for workloads that require high-performance processing as well as the execution of bespoke user-defined functions (UDFs) within Snowflake.

Snowpark Optimized Warehouse supports the execution of custom UDFs written in languages such as Java, Scala, and Kotlin. This feature allows data engineers and data scientists to build custom logic, such as machine learning model inference, directly into Snowflake. This mode is intended to handle more computationally difficult data processing activities, such as data purification, feature engineering, and complicated data transformations, which are frequently linked to machine learning workflows.

Snowpark allows users to design and execute custom functions in popular programming languages, increasing the flexibility and extensibility of Snowflake's data processing capabilities.

Snowpark Optimized Warehouse provides resources optimized for CPU-bound workloads, ensuring that ML and data processing jobs receive adequate computing power for efficient execution. Snowpark functionality interfaces smoothly with prominent ML and AI libraries, allowing data scientists to use their favorite tools and libraries right within Snowflake.

Snowpark Optimized Warehouse Improves ML Processing: Snowpark Optimized Warehouse is especially beneficial for ML processing processes. Data scientists can use Snowflake to deploy bespoke ML models written in languages like Java or Scala as UDFs. This allows for real-time ML model inference within the Snowflake environment.

Complex feature engineering operations, which are frequently critical in ML, can be executed effectively utilizing custom UDFs within Snowflake's Snowpark Optimized Warehouse. ML datasets frequently necessitate considerable preparation. Snowpark allows users to build unique data preparation pipelines to ensure that data is properly processed and cleaned prior to model training. Snowpark makes data integration activities easier by allowing data scientists to seamlessly merge, connect, and alter datasets within Snowflake. This is very helpful when integrating many data sources for ML model training.

Snowpark Optimized Warehouse has the scalability of handling large-scale ML processing jobs, allowing for the higher computational needs that are frequently associated with ML training and inference.

Snowpark ensures that ML processing activities are done efficiently, decreasing processing times and enhancing model training performance by optimizing resource allocation for CPU-bound workloads.

Companies can use Snowflake's Snowpark Optimized Warehouse to run ML models in real-time, allowing for fast predictions and recommendations in their apps and services. Snowpark can be used by data scientists and analysts for sophisticated data analysis, enabling data-driven decision-making procedures that incorporate ML insights, It can be used to construct, train, and deploy predictive ML models directly within Snowflake, greatly simplifying the process of incorporating ML into analytics operations. ML jobs that require large-scale data processing, Snowpark delivers the computational resources required to efficiently process and analyze big datasets.

Snowpark lets enterprises create ML pipelines within Snowflake, ranging from data intake and preprocessing to model training and deployment. Snowpark allows data scientists to connect external ML libraries and tools to Snowflake, allowing them to use their favorite ML frameworks for model training and evaluation.

The integration of Snowpark within Snowflake speeds up the ML workflow, reducing the need to send data to external environments for processing. Snowpark Optimized Warehouse allocates resources that are optimized for CPU-bound tasks, providing efficient processing and shortening query execution times. By conducting ML processes within Snowflake, businesses can save money on data transport, storage, and upkeep of external ML infrastructure.

Snowpark's scalability allows it to handle large-scale ML applications while accommodating expanding datasets and processing demands. Data scientists can construct ML models using their preferred programming languages and ML libraries, providing flexibility and customization. Snowpark allows real-time ML model inference, allowing enterprises to give end-users rapid forecasts and insights.

While Snowpark improves performance, enterprises should keep resource costs in mind, especially when running resource-intensive ML applications. Custom UDFs created in languages such as Java or Scala may require continual maintenance and optimization. Integrating external ML libraries and tools into Snowflake using Snowpark may necessitate some code creation and integration.

Snowpark Optimized Warehouse from Snowflake is a strong resource allocation option designed to support complicated data processing operations such as ML and AI workloads. It lets data engineers, data scientists, and analysts do advanced data transformations, analytics, and machine learning (ML) modeling within the Snowflake platform, thereby enhancing efficiency, performance, and integration.

Snowpark provides enterprises with flexibility, scalability, and resource efficiency, making it a powerful tool for streamlining ML processing workflows and leveraging data-driven insights within their data warehouse.

Snowflake Warehouse Cache

Snowflake's Warehouse Cache is an important part of the company's cloud data warehousing architecture, designed to improve query performance, minimize latency, and optimize data retrieval. This cache is directly incorporated with the virtual warehouses that run queries, allowing for efficient data caching and reuse. In this section, we'll look at the Warehouse Cache, how it adjusts to different warehouse sizes, and how it can be used to create a local cache that greatly improves queries on the same table.

The Warehouse Cache is a cache layer that is included in Snowflake's virtual warehouses. Its principal duty is to store and manage data that has recently been accessed, query results, and intermediate results. This cached data is stored in memory, making it available for subsequent requests without the need to re-scan or re-fetch the same data from storage. The Warehouse Cache enhances query performance dramatically by lowering the time required to access data.

The Warehouse Cache provides speedy data retrieval by keeping frequently requested data and query results in memory, resulting in faster query execution times. As a result, the user experience becomes more responsive and efficient, it eliminates the need to fetch data from slower storage tiers, such as object storage or data lakes, and the Warehouse Cache drastically reduces data access latency. This is especially useful for analytical workloads involving enormous datasets. The Warehouse Cache can be used by multiple queries executing on the same virtual warehouse at the same time. This enables effective resource sharing and increases query concurrency, data is cached in memory, and frequent access to the underlying storage layers is reduced. This means decreased data transit and storage costs, particularly in cloud-based environments.

Users can specify caching policies in Snowflake based on individual use cases and workload requirements. This level of customization ensures that the cache runs in accordance with the parameters of the workload. The Warehouse Cache ensures data coherency by ensuring that cached data remains consistent with the underlying data, even as it changes. This is critical for obtaining accurate query results.

Warehouse Cache's behavior changes dynamically to the size of the virtual warehouse in use. Due to resource limits, the Warehouse Cache is typically smaller in size in smaller warehouses. It does, however, offer advantages by caching frequently requested data, query results, and intermediate calculations. This improves query performance for lighter workloads. As the size of the virtual warehouse grows, so does the Warehouse Cache's capacity. Larger caches can be accommodated in medium-sized warehouses, allowing for more data to be stored in memory. This improves query response times, especially for medium-sized workloads.

The Warehouse Cache can be substantially larger in larger warehouses, allowing for the caching of considerable chunks of frequently accessed data and query results. This improves query performance for large workloads with large data volumes. Snowflake's auto-sizing functionality automatically modifies warehouse size based on query demand. In such instances, the Warehouse Cache scales to match the size of the warehouse at the time, ensuring that available resources are used appropriately.

The Warehouse Cache is like a local cache within each virtual warehouse. The Warehouse Cache ensures that queries conducted on the same virtual warehouse access cached data in a consistent manner. This consistency is important for applications that rely on current, queryable data. Users can configure caching policies based on their individual use cases. Organizations can use this adjustment to match the local cache to their specific workload requirements, the Warehouse Cache reduces the requirement for data movement between storage tiers, and data transmission costs and latency are decreased. This is especially useful in cloud-based systems where data transfer costs can be high.

Since cached data may be retrieved practically instantly, query response times are considerably improved. This is especially useful for queries on huge datasets or data that are often accessed. Queries on the same table within a virtual warehouse can benefit from the Warehouse Cache in a variety of ways, including Query Speed: Subsequent queries on the same table obtain cached data rapidly, resulting in faster query execution. This is especially useful for dashboards, analytics, and reporting applications that query the same dataset repeatedly. Cached data reduces the need for frequent data scans and resource-intensive processing, allowing for more efficient resource utilization within the virtual warehouse. This allows for more concurrent queries and more efficient resource sharing.

Queries on the same table enjoy low-latency access to cached data on a consistent basis, giving a consistent and predictable user experience. This is especially important for applications where query response times have a direct impact on customer satisfaction and, by lowering the amount of data scanned and the compute resources required for query execution, the Warehouse Cache can result in cost savings. Organizations only pay for the time and resources used to perform queries, resulting in cost-effective data analytics.

It is important to monitor cache hit rates and cache capacity on a regular basis to determine how well the Warehouse Cache is performing for your individual workloads, and also recognize and optimize query patterns in your workloads. Query structure that aligns with common access patterns improves cache hit rates and performance. Configure caching policies that are appropriate for your individual use cases. By customizing these policies, you may ensure that the Warehouse Cache performs optimally for your workloads. Align data loading and changes with cache management algorithms. Understanding when cache invalidations occur is critical for data coherency.

Snowflake's Warehouse Cache is an effective solution for improving query performance, lowering latency, and improving data retrieval. It dynamically adapts to the size of the virtual warehouse and provides major benefits for constructing a local cache that significantly increases query performance, particularly for queries on the same table. The Warehouse Cache, with its flexibility, scalability, and customization possibilities, enables enterprises to deliver faster and more efficient data analytics solutions while optimizing cloud computing costs.

Snowflake Query Cache

The Query Cache feature in Snowflake improves query performance by storing and reusing the results of previously completed queries. It's an important part of Snowflake's overall performance optimization approach, aiming to improve query response times, lowering computing costs, and improving the overall user experience. In this detailed section, we'll look at the Query Cache in-depth, learn how it works, and highlight its benefits, particularly in instances involving the same or similar queries.

The Query Cache is a specialized cache within Snowflake that holds the results of previously conducted SQL queries. When a user submits a query, Snowflake checks the Query Cache to verify if the identical question has already been cached. If a cached result exists and meets specific conditions, Snowflake returns it rather than re-executing the query. This caching strategy aids in the reduction of query execution times and associated computational expenses.

The fundamental advantage of the Query Cache is faster query execution. When a query is served from the cache, the response time is virtually instantaneous because the result is not recomputed. As a result, the user experience becomes more responsive and efficient. By reusing cached results, Snowflake decreases the requirement for processing resources to re-execute identical searches. This corresponds to cheaper cloud computing costs, particularly for workloads involving repetitive or recurring requests.

The Query Cache improves query concurrency by swiftly providing cached results. This means that numerous users or programs can run the same query at the same time without overloading the system. Even during peak workloads, users may expect consistent query performance. Queries that are conducted frequently and have their results cached consistently have low-latency response times.

Snowflake's Query Cache offloads query processing from compute clusters, freeing up resources for more sophisticated or unique queries. This keeps clusters available for other work and avoids resource contention. Snowflake handles the Query Cache automatically, including cache invalidation when the underlying data changes. This removes the need for manual cache management while also ensuring cache accuracy.

The same queries are frequently conducted again in organizations where regular reports are generated. The Query Cache saves and provides the findings of these reports, which reduces query response times and ensures efficient report production. Dashboards that are frequently used by several users who have access to the same underlying datasets benefit from a query cache and by supplying cached results for frequently accessed queries, the Query Cache can considerably improve dashboard load times.

Workloads frequently display query patterns in which the same or similar queries are run with various parameters. By spotting patterns and serving stored results, the Query Cache can speed up these searches. The Query Cache can benefit identical or comparable queries even in ad hoc query situations. When users re-run prior queries or variations on them, the cached results can be returned rapidly. When exploring datasets, data analysts and scientists may regularly perform similar queries while experimenting with different analytical methodologies. The Query Cache guarantees that these exploratory queries respond quickly and do not take too many resources.

Snowflake uniquely identifies each question by using a hash of the query content, its accompanying metadata, and session-specific information. This hash is used as the cache key for the query.

When a query is filed, Snowflake checks the Query Cache to see if a cached result for the same query key exists. If a match is found, Snowflake looks at other criteria to see if the cached result can be used. Snowflake uses a number of criteria to evaluate cache eligibility. These include making sure the cache isn't outdated (that is to make sure, the underlying data hasn't changed since the cached result was formed) and that the cached result is consistent with the user's session context (for example, acceptable access permissions).

Snowflake receives a cached result from the Query Cache and returns it to the user if it fits all requirements. If not, the query is run normally, and the result may be cached for later use.

When the underlying data changes, Snowflake automatically invalidates cached results, maintaining data accuracy and preventing the serving of outdated results.

It is always a best practice to Keep an eye on cache hit rates and cache size to see how well the Query Cache is performing for your workload. If your queries have parameters, put them in the query text to maximize cache reuse. varying cache keys are generated by queries with varying parameters. Recognize query patterns in your workload and arrange queries to take advantage of caching. Reusing typical query patterns can result in increased cache hit rates.

Make certain that your data management methods, such as data loading and updates, are consistent with your cache management strategy. It is critical to understand when cache invalidations occur. When utilizing the Query Cache, keep session-specific variables and settings in mind. Because cached results are linked to certain session contexts, make sure that these contexts match the needs of the user.

Snowflake's Query Cache is a useful tool for optimizing query performance, lowering computation costs, and increasing overall user experience. The Query Cache reduces query response times and benefits identical or similar questions by storing and providing the results of previously conducted queries. Cost reductions, enhanced query concurrency, and consistent performance across data warehousing workloads should be expected, making Snowflake's Query Cache as a crucial tool for improving query execution in the cloud.

Conclusion

Finally, because of its unique and strong features, Snowflake's data warehousing solution stands out in the competitive market of cloud-based data management. Its unrivaled capacity to scale dynamically is one of its most outstanding features, making it a great choice for enterprises of all sizes and industries.

The architecture of Snowflake and its resource allocation features, such as Warehouse Scaling Policies and Warehouse Maximized Mode, demonstrate its adaptability to different workloads and commitment to performance improvement. Snowflake's separation of computing and storage is one of its most notable characteristics, allowing enterprises to expand these resources independently. This separation enhances efficiency since storage can be easily scaled up or down as data volumes vary, whereas computing resources may be allocated flexibly to match query requirements. This architecture ensures that enterprises never overpay for resources they don't require, which is a key feature of Snowflake's cost-effectiveness.

In addition, Snowflake's Warehouse Scaling Policies provide a more complex approach to resource allocation. The Economy Policy strikes a balance between cost containment and acceptable query performance, whereas the Standard Policy maintains a responsive query environment that can handle general-purpose workloads. Snowflake's commitment to balancing cost reduction and performance optimization is exemplified by these policies.

Warehouse Maximized Mode, on the other hand, displays Snowflake's commitment to delivering outstanding performance in situations where performance is critical, even if it means paying a higher price. This resource allocation method is appropriate for sophisticated data processing operations, such as Machine Learning processes, where speed is critical.

Snowflake's unique query timeout feature distinguishes it further by providing an important tool for query management. This feature enables businesses to establish maximum query execution periods, preventing runaway queries from monopolizing resources and reducing system performance. It is a necessary component for ensuring a smooth and responsive query environment.

The Snowpark Optimized Warehouse, which enables advanced data processing tasks such as the execution of custom user-defined functions (UDFs) in languages such as Java and Scala, is another distinguishing feature of Snowflake's architecture. This feature increases Snowflake's adaptability and agility to a variety of data processing jobs, particularly in the realms of Machine Learning and AI.

To summarize, Snowflake's data warehousing solution is distinguished by its own architecture and features that prioritize scalability, performance optimization, and cost-efficiency. Because of its capacity to dynamically scale resources independent of computing and storage, it is a versatile alternative for enterprises with diverse workloads. Among the outstanding features that cater to a wide range of data processing needs are the Warehouse Scaling Policies, Warehouse Maximized Mode, query timeout, and Snowpark Optimized Warehouse. Snowflake's dedication to innovation and adaptability distinguishes it as a premier cloud data warehousing solution capable of serving the broad and developing needs of modern data-driven enterprises.

In the chapter that comes next, we'll look at Snowflake's role-based access management and how it may be used to manage secure user access in large enterprises.

References

- https://docs.snowflake.com/en/user-guide/querying-persisted-results
- https://www.linkedin.com/pulse/snowflake-concurrency-parallel-processing-subhrajit-bandyopadhyay

CHAPTER 4

Role-Based Access Control

Introduction

In Snowflake, role-based access control (RBAC) is critical for constructing a safe and well-managed data environment. RBAC provides a flexible and granular way to control user permissions and access within the Snowflake cloud data platform, ensuring that users have enough access to data and resources. RBAC in Snowflake starts with the establishment and maintenance of roles. Roles are used to group people and define shared permissions. Administrators can define roles and assign them to users to create a hierarchical access privilege structure.

Snowflake's RBAC functionalities include permission granting and revocation. Granular permissions can be granted to roles by administrators, allowing them to specify which actions can be performed on certain objects or data. In turn, they can remove rights when they are no longer required, ensuring that users only have access to the resources they require.

To ensure an effective RBAC installation, Snowflake provides best practices for role-based access control. This comprises role organization, authorization definition and management, and role inheritance. Following these best practices ensures a streamlined and safe access control architecture. Snowflake RBAC cannot exist without role administration and auditing. Administrators can manage role allocations, change role hierarchies, and monitor role actions. Audit logging capabilities improve compliance, governance, and security by allowing the tracking of role modifications, user designations, and role-based access events.

By implementing RBAC in Snowflake and following best practices for role creation, permission management, and role auditing, organizations can develop a comprehensive and secure access control architecture. Snowflake's RBAC provides a scalable and adaptive solution for managing user access, ensuring data security, and platform compliance.

Structure

In this chapter, the following topics to be covered:

- Introduction to Role-Based Access Control (RBAC)
- Creating and Managing Roles
- Permission Granting and Revocation
- Role-Based Access Control Best Practices
- Role Management and Auditing

Introduction to Role-Based Access Control

Role-Based Access Control (RBAC) is a basic notion in Snowflake's data security and access management framework. RBAC is a way of managing and regulating access to resources within Snowflake based on preset roles and privileges. In this section, we'll look at the importance of RBAC in Snowflake and how it improves data security and governance.

RBAC is a hierarchical framework in Snowflake that sets and enforces permissions for users, roles, and objects (such as databases, tables, and views) within the data warehouse. RBAC is based on the notion that permissions are granted to roles rather than to individual users. Users are then assigned roles and inherit the permissions associated with those roles.

Snowflake's RBAC key components are as follows:

Roles: Snowflake's RBAC framework revolves around roles. They are predetermined sets of permissions that can be provided to users. Roles can be arranged hierarchically, with parent roles carrying a subset of the permissions of their child roles.

Users: Users are individual accounts that have access to Snowflake. Users can be allocated to one or more roles, which govern their level of access and the tasks they can conduct within the system.

Privileges: Privileges are precise permissions that specify what activities can be performed on Snowflake objects. Privileges, for example, can allow the power to select data from a table or establish a new database.

RBAC enables granular control over who can access and change data. This guarantees that users only have the permissions required for their roles and responsibilities. RBAC scales well, making it simple to handle rights for an increasing number of users and objects in the data warehouse. RBAC improves data security by lowering the risk of unauthorized access and data breaches. It ensures that users can only conduct actions that they are specifically authorized to perform. RBAC assists organizations in meeting regulatory and compliance obligations by providing a structured approach to access control and auditability.

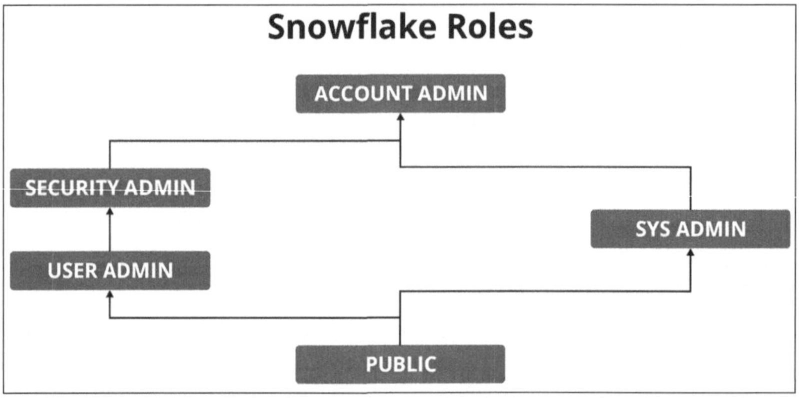

***Figure 4.1**: Snowflake Roles Hierarchy*

RBAC streamlines access control policy administration and lowers administrative overhead by arranging permissions into roles and hierarchies.

Snowflake has various preconfigured roles that cover common use cases. The most prevalent roles are:

- **`ORGADMIN`:** The **`ORGADMIN`** role manages data and features for all organization accounts. This role allows tasks such as listing all accounts and creating new ones.
- **`ACCOUNTADMIN`:** This role is in charge of managing the Snowflake account, including billing and account settings.
- **`SYSADMIN`:** This is a powerful role, often assigned to administrators who have complete control over the Snowflake environment.
- **`SECURITYADMIN`:** Users with this role can manage security-related features such as creating and managing roles and allocating rights.
- **Database `READER`, `WRITER`, and `ADMIN` roles:** These roles are frequently used to control access to certain databases within Snowflake.
- **`PUBLIC`:** All users are implicitly members of the PUBLIC role. By default, permissions provided to **`PUBLIC`** apply to all users.

RBAC is a fundamental component of Snowflake's data security and access control strategy. It provides a standardized and scalable solution to managing who can access and alter data within the Snowflake environment. Organizations may assure data security, compliance, and effective access control policy management by giving roles and privileges to users.

Creating and managing roles in Snowflake is a critical component of data warehouse access control and security. Roles define sets of permissions that govern what actions users can take on Snowflake objects. They are an essential component of Snowflake's Role-Based Access Control (RBAC) system, allowing enterprises to effectively enforce security and governance standards. In the next section, we'll look at how to establish, manage, and best practices for roles in Snowflake.

Creating and Managing Roles

Roles are created by users with the proper credentials, usually administrators such as `USERADMIN` or `SECURITYADMIN`.

Once created, roles can be managed in order to grant or withdraw privileges and control access. The following are the primary management tasks for roles. Snowflake provides a role hierarchy in which roles can inherit privileges from other roles. This simplifies and improves the efficiency of role management. Maintaining a secure and well-organized data environment requires effective role management.

Here are some examples of best practices:

- **Role creation**: To decrease the danger of unauthorized access, assign users roles with the bare minimum of privileges.
- **Organization of roles**: To increase clarity and organization, use meaningful and consistent naming conventions for roles. Use terms like *analyst*, *developer*, or *admin*.
- **Role review:** Review and audit jobs and their related rights on a regular basis to ensure security and compliance.
- **Documentation of roles:** Describe the purpose and responsibilities of each role. This facilitates role administration and assists users in understanding their permissions.
- **Role revocation**: To decrease clutter and potential security issues, remove roles that are no longer required.

The ability to create and manage roles in Snowflake is critical for keeping a safe, organized, and compliant data environment. Organizations can utilize roles to limit access, enforce security standards, and simplify user privilege management. Organizations can establish a robust access control system within Snowflake by following best practices and assessing roles on a regular basis, supporting their data security and governance objectives.

Permission Granting and Revocation

Roles are created by users with the proper credentials, usually administrators such as **USERADMIN** or **SECURITYADMIN**.

Ensuring the security of data has become a matter of utmost importance for enterprises in the contemporary digital era. The Snowflake database management system is a cloud-based platform designed for data warehousing. It provides a comprehensive set of capabilities that enable efficient administration of data access through a highly structured and detailed permission system. The act of granting and revoking permissions in Snowflake is of utmost importance in safeguarding data security, guaranteeing compliance, and facilitating efficient data governance.

The process of providing permission in Snowflake is a rigorous procedure that enables data managers to allocate different levels of access to individuals, roles, and objects within the database. The use of precise control mechanisms allows enterprises to develop a data-sharing ecosystem that is both secure and efficient.

Snowflake provides administrators with the capability to allocate rights at the object level, specifically for tables, views, and databases. Users may be granted rights such as **SELECT**, **INSERT**, **UPDATE**, and **DELETE**, which are crucial for efficient data processing. Role-Based Access Control (RBAC) is an essential aspect of permission management in Snowflake, as roles play a critical role in this process. Roles are allocated permissions, and users are linked to these roles. The utilization of a role-based approach facilitates the management process and guarantees consistent access controls among various user groups.

In the context of user management, permissions have the capability to be inherited in a hierarchical manner, hence facilitating the effective administration of extensive user populations. When a role is bestowed with specific privileges, all users who are assigned to that role acquire those privileges, hence diminishing the necessity for repetitive permission assignments. The utilization of stored procedures is facilitated by Snowflake, enabling administrators to construct encapsulated entities that contain intricate logic for accessing and manipulating data. Organizations can effectively uphold data security and simultaneously enable access to robust data processing capabilities by implementing permissions at the stored procedure level.

The act of granting permission is of utmost importance, but it is as crucial to consider the process of revoking permission in order to effectively respond to evolving data access demands and uphold a strong security stance. Snowflake provides the capability to remove permissions as required, which is crucial for ensuring effective data governance.

The concept of granular revocation allows administrators to selectively revoke permissions at different levels, such as object, role, or user, in order to ensure that only the required access privileges are retained. The use of fine-grained control mitigates the potential for unauthorized data exposure. The revocation of permits results in an immediate implementation. This particular feature proves to be highly advantageous in situations where prompt response to security issues or frequent alterations in access criteria are necessary.

Snowflake has robust auditing and monitoring functionalities, which empower administrators to effectively monitor and manage modifications to permissions. The maintenance of data security and adherence to regulatory obligations necessitates the utmost importance of visibility. In summary, the act of giving and revoking permissions within the Snowflake database management system plays a crucial role in ensuring data security, governance, and compliance.

Snowflake's methodology of implementing a fine-grained system for rights management, utilizing RBAC and enabling prompt revocation of privileges, equips enterprises with the necessary resources to safeguard their data assets and guarantee efficient management of access to sensitive information. By adopting these characteristics, enterprises may utilize Snowflake's robust data warehousing functionalities while upholding the utmost standards of data security and governance, thereby cultivating trust and assurance in their data operations.

Role-Based Access Control Best Practices

Role-Based Access Control (RBAC) is a pivotal security mechanism within Snowflake, a cloud-based data warehousing platform, which empowers enterprises to effectively administer and regulate data access with meticulousness. The use of RBAC best practices in Snowflake is crucial for maintaining data security, mitigating the potential for data breaches, and facilitating efficient data governance. This section aims to examine the essential best practices of RBAC in the context of Snowflake.

The establishment of well-organized role hierarchies is a crucial preliminary measure in the implementation of RBAC within the Snowflake platform. Roles are employed as a means of categorizing users and bestowing them with specific privileges, while the hierarchy establishes the interrelationships between these roles. An illustration of potential responsibilities within an organization could include designations such as Analyst, Data Scientist, and Administrator. Designing a logical hierarchy that accurately represents the organizational structure and access requirements is of utmost importance.

The adherence to the least privilege concept entails the allocation of the minimum level of permissions required for users and roles to carry out their designated duties. Snowflake has a comprehensive permission system that enables users to define precise permissions for various actions, like **`SELECT`**, **`INSERT`**, and **`DELETE`**, on specific objects. It is advisable to refrain from excessively privileging roles, as doing so can decrease the likelihood of unwanted access or manipulation of data.

Grouping users into roles is a recommended approach for managing permissions, as opposed to providing rights to individual users. This practice entails categorizing users based on their respective duties and access needs. This streamlines the process of managing permissions and decreases the administrative burden. An instance of a Finance Analyst role may be established, which confers restricted access solely for the purpose of viewing financial information.

It is advisable to do periodic evaluations and assessments of the roles and permissions within your Snowflake environment in order to revoke access privileges as necessary. It is imperative to swiftly remove the authorization of users when they undergo role changes or depart from the organization. Snowflake provides the capability to revoke rights at many levels, including the object level, role level, and user level, guaranteeing that access privileges remain current and accurate.

Snowflake provides a wide range of auditing and monitoring capabilities. Enabling auditing is recommended in order to monitor and record alterations in permissions and access patterns. It is advisable to maintain vigilance in order to detect any potentially illicit actions, such as an abrupt increase in data retrieval. These activities serve to bolster security measures and aid in the detection of potential security vulnerabilities.

One might consider utilizing Snowflake's stored procedures in order to encapsulate intricate logic for data access and modification. Enhanced security can be achieved by exercising control over the execution of procedures through the granting of permissions at the procedure level.

The process of data classification and labeling involves categorizing data according to its level of sensitivity, such as public, confidential, or highly sensitive. Data labeling is a technique employed to implement distinct access controls for various categories of data. The RBAC framework developed by Snowflake has the capability to incorporate data classification policies as an extension.

Regular training and awareness initiatives should be implemented to educate both users and administrators on the principles and implementation of RBAC as well as the adoption of best practices in this regard. It is imperative for users to possess a comprehensive understanding of their respective roles and associated duties. Similarly, administrators must possess a thorough comprehension of the potential consequences that may arise from granting specific rights. The presence of this awareness diminishes the probability of inadvertent data leaks.

The process of integrating Snowflake with an organization's identity provider (IdP) enables the implementation of single sign-on (SSO) and multi-factor authentication (MFA) functionalities. By implementing this measure, an additional level of protection is established, guaranteeing that only individuals with proper authorization are able to obtain entry to the Snowflake system.

One potential strategy to enhance role management is the implementation of automation for the assignment and revocation of roles. The utilization of tools and scripts can effectively contribute to the consistent management of permissions, hence mitigating the potential for manual errors.

Regular security assessments should be conducted periodically to discover vulnerabilities and potential concerns in the implementation of RBAC. This can be achieved through the use of security assessments and penetration testing. The implementation of a proactive strategy aids in the identification and resolution of security vulnerabilities prior to their exploitation.

In summary, Role-Based Access Control (RBAC) within the Snowflake platform serves as a robust system for upholding data security, managing access control, and ensuring governance. By adhering to these recommended practices for Role-Based Access Control (RBAC), companies may establish a resilient and effective security framework that not only safeguards their confidential information but also facilitates adherence to regulatory obligations.

The integration of RBAC with Snowflake's comprehensive permission system, auditing functionalities, and monitoring capabilities guarantees effective management of data access, hence mitigating the potential for data breaches and upholding confidence in the organization's data handling protocols.

Snowflake employs groups, roles, and users as fundamental elements of its access and security framework. The following are a few specific examples that demonstrate the interconnectedness of various entities in real-time. Within a large company that encompasses many divisions, such as Sales, Marketing, and Finance, it is necessary to establish distinct groups for each department (for example, `Sales_Group`, `Marketing_Group`) and allocate appropriate users to these groups in order to grant access to certain datasets. Specify the appropriate privileges for each role, such as **`Sales_Analyst`** and **`Marketing_Analyst`**. Allocate roles to corresponding groups, guaranteeing that users get access privileges according to their departmental affiliation.

To enforce access control for various levels of data within an organization, the implementation of RBAC is necessary. This involves defining specific roles such as **`Data_Analyst`**, **`Data_Scientist`**, and **`Data_Administrator`**. Allocate distinct rights to various roles, mirroring the precise level of access that each role should possess. Next, allocate users to suitable roles according to their respective duties. This guarantees that users receive the permissions linked to their responsibilities. Occasionally, an organization may engage in collaborations with external partners that need access to certain datasets. In such cases, a Partner role can be established, granting restricted privileges that enable access only to the essential data. Allocate external users to this role. In order to categorize the users, establish a **`Partner_Group`** and include the external users within this group. This guarantees that external partners are granted regulated access to the necessary data while maintaining the integrity of security measures.

Role Management and Auditing

Snowflake is widely recognized in the field of data management for its exceptional cloud-based data warehousing platform, which is highly regarded for its comprehensive role management and auditing functionalities. Role management and auditing are essential components in maintaining data security, facilitating appropriate access to authorized individuals, and guaranteeing compliance with relevant requirements. This section aims to examine the role-management and auditing capabilities of Snowflake and elucidate their significance in contributing to the platform's overall effectiveness.

The concept of role management refers to the practice of organizing and assigning various roles within an organization or database account. It involves the identification,

Role management in Snowflake includes the procedural aspects of establishing, allocating, and overseeing roles that govern the authorization to access the database and its associated entities. Role-based access control (RBAC) is a robust approach utilized to uphold data security and guarantee that data is exclusively accessed by individuals with approved privileges. Snowflake encompasses several fundamental elements pertaining to role management.

The Snowflake platform facilitates the establishment of a hierarchical structure for roles. This architectural framework streamlines the administrative process by allowing roles to inherit permissions from pre-existing roles. This implies that roles situated at higher levels of the hierarchy have the ability to assign access control responsibilities to roles positioned beneath them, thus establishing a streamlined and efficient method for managing access.

Snowflake provides a granular privilege assignment mechanism that allows for the precise allocation of rights at many levels, including roles, databases, schemas, and objects. The implementation of granular control enables administrators to customize access privileges according to the specific requirements of their business.

Role inheritance is a mechanism by which users are assigned certain responsibilities, and subsequently acquire the permissions associated with those roles. This approach streamlines the process of managing users and guarantees the uniform implementation of rights across various user groups.

Snowflake offers default privileges for each type of item, facilitating the granting of fundamental access to users while upholding stringent security measures.

Snowflake offers dynamic data masking as an additional feature alongside standard role management. This functionality facilitates the dynamic masking of sensitive data based on user privileges, guaranteeing that even users with elevated privileges are limited to viewing only the material they have been granted authorization to access.

The process of auditing involves the systematic examination and evaluation of enterprise wide user access, the practice of auditing of auditing plays a vital role in guaranteeing security and adherence to regulatory requirements inside a data management platform. Snowflake provides comprehensive auditing features that enable enterprises to effectively monitor and manage activities occurring within their database environment.

Snowflake maintains an extensive logging system that captures various activities, encompassing login attempts, executed queries, modifications to privileges, and other relevant events. The preceding logs offer a comprehensive account of all activities occurring within the database.

The system allows administrators to create personalized auditing policies, enabling them to determine the specific activities that should be subject to auditing and the individuals for whom such audits are applicable. The presence of flexibility in auditing processes guarantees that the alignment between auditing activities and the unique requirements and compliance mandates of the company is maintained.

Snowflake provides businesses with the capability to establish policies governing the duration for which audit data is preserved. Ensuring compliance with data retention rules and efficiently controlling storage expenses are of utmost importance.

Access to Audit Data: Individuals possessing the necessary credentials are able to retrieve audit data, enabling them to conduct inquiries into security incidents, resolve problems, and provide evidence of adherence to regulatory requirements during audit processes.

The integration of Snowflake's audit data with third-party security information and event management (SIEM) technologies enables the convenient consolidation of audit logs for centralized monitoring and analysis.

In summary, the role management and auditing functionalities offered by Snowflake are crucial in upholding data security, guaranteeing adherence to regulatory requirements, and effectively overseeing data access within the platform. The use of role-based access control and role hierarchy functionalities empowers companies to establish a systematic and expandable framework for managing access. The auditing capabilities, in the meantime, offer transparency, accountability, and the capacity to efficiently address security events or meet compliance obligations. By utilizing these characteristics, enterprises can effectively utilize the capabilities of Snowflake for their data warehousing requirements while ensuring the protection and confidentiality of their data.

Conclusion

In summary, this chapter pertaining to *Role-Based Access Control* (RBAC) *in Snowflake* has presented a thorough examination of the fundamental elements of data security and access administration within the Snowflake database. A variety of subjects have been examined, commencing with an overview of Role-Based Access Control (RBAC), which serves as the fundamental principle for managing resource access in Snowflake. RBAC enables businesses to effectively enforce permissions and access regulations, hence facilitating the secure administration of data.

We explored the pragmatic elements of RBAC encompassing the establishment and administration of roles. During the course, we acquired knowledge on the process of role creation, permission granting, and revocation, as well as the establishment of role hierarchies. The implementation of these steps is crucial for the establishment of a well-structured and organized access control system.

In addition, the topic of permission granting and revocation was deliberated, with a particular emphasis placed on the need to stick to the concept of least privilege. This approach is designed to guarantee that users and roles are granted just the rights that are essential for carrying out their respective obligations. By doing so, it mitigates the potential for unauthorized access or security breaches.

The chapter presented an extensive compilation of optimal methodologies for RBAC furnishing valuable recommendations on the efficient implementation and ongoing maintenance of robust access control measures. The use of best practices, such as the utilization of role naming conventions, conducting frequent audits, and maintaining comprehensive role documentation, plays a crucial part in the establishment of a resilient security architecture.

The topics of role management and auditing were thoroughly examined and analyzed in this chapter. The implementation of effective role management encompasses the establishment of roles with well-defined objectives, the allocation of responsibilities to users, and the consistent upkeep of documentation and periodic evaluations. In contrast, auditing serves the purpose of enabling enterprises to effectively oversee access, monitor user actions, and guarantee adherence to security regulations. The maintenance of a secure and well-organized data environment necessitates the inclusion of both role management and auditing as crucial components.

To conclude, the chapter has provided readers with the necessary knowledge and resources for the efficient implementation and administration of RBAC within the Snowflake database. Organizations can achieve a harmonious equilibrium between data accessibility and security by adhering to the recommended guidelines presented in this chapter. This approach guarantees that users and roles are granted suitable access privileges while simultaneously mitigating the potential for unauthorized actions and data breaches. When RBAC is established and managed in a deliberate manner, it serves as a fundamental element of data security and governance within the Snowflake platform, hence playing a significant role in the achievements of data-driven enterprises.

The next chapter will shed light on two key data security and privacy issues in the Snowflake data warehousing technology.

CHAPTER 5

Snowflake Data Governance

Introduction

The implementation and maintenance of data governance practices play a vital role in the management and safeguarding of an organization's data assets. Snowflake is a data platform that operates on cloud infrastructure and provides comprehensive functionalities and capabilities to facilitate data governance endeavors, ensuring reliability, confidentiality, and adherence to regulatory requirements of data.

The data governance framework of Snowflake encompasses various elements, including data classification, access restrictions, data obfuscation, and data lifecycle management. The primary aim is to establish comprehensive rules, methods, and standards for the management, utilization, and safeguarding of data.

The implementation of data obfuscation policies is an essential aspect of Snowflake's data governance framework. Data masking is a technique employed to safeguard sensitive information by replacing it with seemingly valid yet fabricated data. Snowflake has robust data masking functionalities that allow enterprises to establish and implement data masking policies at a granular level, specifically at the column level. This ensures the utmost protection of sensitive data.

The utilization of row access policies constitutes an essential component of data governance inside the Snowflake platform. Row access policies provide a means of exerting precise control over data access by establishing requirements or predicates that dictate which rows of data users are permitted to access. This policy guarantees that solely authorized persons or designated roles possess the capability to retrieve sensitive or restricted data within the organizational framework.

By leveraging Snowflake's data governance capabilities, businesses may develop a comprehensive and compliant data governance framework through the implementation of data concealment policies and row access restrictions. These capabilities enable enterprises to efficiently safeguard sensitive data, control data access, and enforce data governance regulations. The data governance features offered by Snowflake facilitate organizational compliance with regulatory mandates, preservation of data integrity, and establishment of trust in their data assets.

Structure

In this chapter, the following topics to be covered:

- Introduction to Data Governance in Snowflake
- Data Masking policy in Snowflake
- Row Access Policies in Snowflake

Introduction to Data Governance in Snowflake

In the current era characterized by data-driven decision-making, the establishment of efficient data governance is of utmost importance for companies aiming to uphold the confidentiality, integrity, and accessibility of their sensitive data. The emergence of Snowflake, a cloud-based data warehousing platform, has provided a robust solution for the management and security of extensive datasets. Snowflake's data governance capabilities are anchored on its robust features pertaining to the Data Masking policy and Row Access Policy.

Data governance involves a variety of methodologies, regulations, and technological tools that aid organizations in effectively managing their data resources. Its primary objective is to ensure the responsible and secure utilization of data while adhering to regulatory requirements. Snowflake, due to its distinctive architectural design, offers a data warehousing solution that is both scalable and high-performing. Additionally, it gives customers a comprehensive set of tools to ensure effective data governance. Data Masking and Row Access Policies are essential technologies that have a significant impact on maintaining data privacy and security inside the Snowflake ecosystem.

Data masking policies enable enterprises to disguise confidential information within a database, thereby safeguarding against unwanted access by individuals or programs. This attribute holds significant value in situations involving Personally Identifiable Information (PII) or sensitive financial data. The ability to achieve a harmonious equilibrium between data accessibility and data protection poses a recurring challenge for companies operating in a data-centric environment.

In contrast, Row Access Policies provide businesses with the ability to establish precise access control measures for individual data rows within their Snowflake databases. These policies provide administrators with the ability to delineate the individuals who are granted access to particular data rows, contingent upon predetermined criteria. Row Access Policies are essential for upholding data security and privacy, as they facilitate the enforcement of data segregation within several departments and restrict access to key documents exclusively to authorized individuals.

This chapter explores the realm of Data Governance in Snowflake, placing particular emphasis on the topics of Data Masking and Row Access Policies. This chapter aims to examine the potential utilization of these characteristics in order to protect confidential data and regulate data accessibility within the Snowflake data warehouse. Upon completion of this chapter, readers will possess a comprehensive comprehension of the methods for implementing and overseeing these policies with efficacy. Consequently, they will be equipped to bolster their organization's data governance stance inside the constantly expanding realm of data management and security.

Data Masking Policy in Snowflake

Data Masking is a data security technique used to hide or obfuscate sensitive information within a dataset, replacing it with a pseudonym or altered value. The primary objective is to protect the confidentiality of sensitive data, such as personally identifiable information (PII), financial data, or confidential business information, while still allowing legitimate users to access and work with the data.

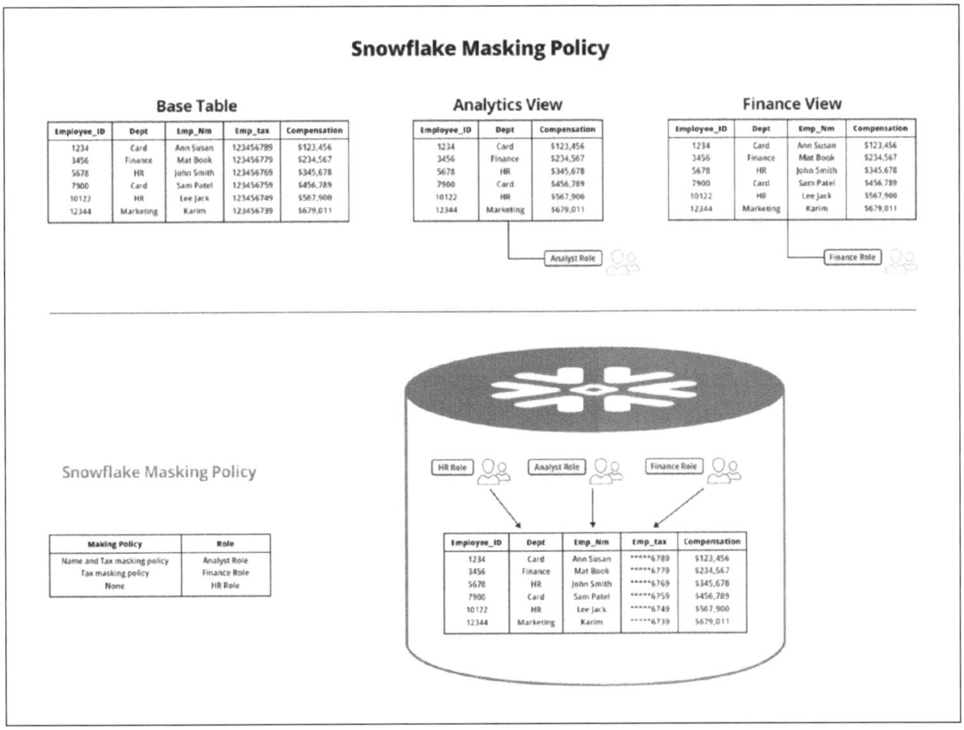

***Figure 5.1**: Snowflake Masking Policy*

The preceding figure demonstrates the application of data masking techniques to enforce restricted access to customer data. In contrast to conventional databases, where multiple views are typically created in Snowflake, the utilization of a masking policy obviates the need for excessive view creation.

Data Masking in Snowflake

In Snowflake, Data Masking is implemented through policies. These policies define the rules for masking specific columns or fields in a table. When a user queries the data, the masking policy is applied, and the user sees the masked values, rather than the original sensitive data.

For example, consider a table containing customer information with columns for social security numbers and credit card numbers. By defining a Data Masking policy, you can ensure that when non-privileged users query the table, these sensitive values are automatically replaced with masked data, like XXX-XX-XXXX for social security numbers or --****-1234 for credit card numbers.

Effective Use of Data Masking in Snowflake

- **Identifying Sensitive Data**: The first step in effective Data Masking is identifying what data needs protection. This includes any information subject to privacy regulations, sensitive business data, or proprietary information.
- **Defining Clear Policies**: Create well-defined Data Masking policies that specify which columns need masking and what type of masking should be applied. Snowflake supports various masking functions, including full masking, partial masking, and custom masking expressions.
- **Role-Based Access Control:** Assign the Data Masking policies based on the roles and permissions of users. Privileged users might see the unmasked data, while others will only view the masked values.
- **Testing and Validation:** Thoroughly test the masking policies in a non-production environment to ensure they work as intended. Verify that sensitive data is effectively protected and that authorized users can still perform their tasks.
- **Monitoring and Auditing**: Regularly monitor and audit the application of Data Masking policies. Snowflake provides audit logs that can help track who accessed the data and what they saw, ensuring compliance with privacy regulations.

Common Mistakes in Data Masking

While Data Masking is a powerful security measure, there are potential pitfalls to watch out for:

- **Over-Masking**: Applying overly restrictive masking policies can render data useless for legitimate analysis. It's essential to strike a balance between data protection and usability.
- **Inadequate Testing:** Failing to thoroughly test masking policies before deploying them in production can lead to unintended data exposure or data that's difficult to work with.
- **Ignoring Data Evolution:** Data changes over time, and masking policies must evolve accordingly. Neglecting to update policies as data schemas change can result in gaps in protection.
- **Misconfigurations:** Incorrectly configured masking policies can lead to data breaches or data that are inadequately protected. Regularly review and validate policy configurations.

Best Practices for Data Masking

To make the most of Data Masking in Snowflake and avoid common pitfalls, consider these best practices:

- **Stay Informed:** Keep up with evolving privacy regulations and adjust your masking policies accordingly to ensure compliance.
- **Regularly Review and Update Policies:** As data evolves and new sensitive fields are identified, update your masking policies to reflect these changes.
- **Education and Training:** Ensure that users and administrators are well-informed about Data Masking policies and their implications. This fosters a culture of data security.
- **Leverage Data Classification:** Classify data based on sensitivity levels, allowing for more granular masking policies. Not all data needs the same level of protection.
- **Use Auditing Tools**: Take advantage of Snowflake's auditing capabilities to monitor data access and ensure that masking policies are effectively applied.

In conclusion, Snowflake's Data Masking policy is a valuable asset for safeguarding sensitive data in an era where data privacy and security are paramount. By understanding how Data Masking works, effectively implementing it, avoiding common pitfalls, and adhering to best practices, organizations can strike the right balance between data protection and usability, ensuring that sensitive data remains confidential while still delivering value to authorized users.

Row Access Policy in Snowflake

In the ever-evolving realm of contemporary data management, the preservation of data security and the implementation of access control measures hold utmost significance. The Row Access Policies offered by Snowflake present a comprehensive and effective approach to achieving precise control over data security. These rules enable businesses to establish the criteria for determining which individuals are granted access to particular rows of data within a table. This provides a detailed level of control over data access, ensuring the preservation of data privacy and compliance with relevant regulations. This detailed tutorial aims to examine the concept of Row Access Policies, their optimal utilization, potential challenges and recommended strategies for optimizing their advantages on the Snowflake platform.

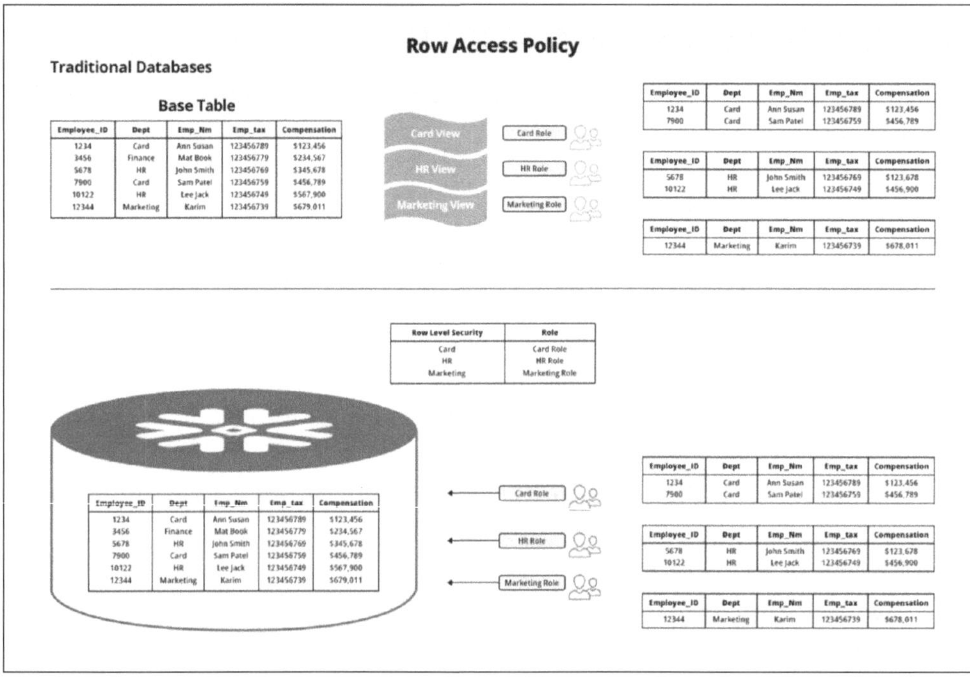

***Figure 5.2**: Row Access Policy*

The preceding figure demonstrates the implementation of a Row access policy, whereby data restriction is based on user profiles. This policy ensures that users are only allowed to read rows inside a table for which they possess authorization. This approach differs from conventional databases, where the creation of views is typically required.

Understanding Row Access Policies

Row Access Policies, commonly known as Row-Level Security (RLS), are a functionality present in Snowflake that enables businesses to exercise control over data access at the granular level within a table. Row Access Policies allow for the specification of established criteria to determine which rows of data individual users or roles can access, in contrast to the conventional access controls that operate at the table or column level.

Row Access Policies function by establishing regulations that selectively restrict access to specific rows within a given table. The aforementioned rules are linked to certain users or roles and are assessed during runtime when data is requested. When a user's query satisfies the conditions specified in a Row Access Policy, they are granted access to the associated rows. Conversely, if the query fails to meet the set criteria, those rows are concealed and not visible to the user.

An illustrative case involves a healthcare database containing patient records. Row Access Policies are implemented to enforce restrictions on the ability of medical personnel to retrieve patient records, thereby mitigating the risk of unlawful access to confidential patient information.

Effective Use of Row Access Policies in Snowflake

- The initial stage in the implementation of Row Access Policies is the identification of data that necessitates precise and detailed access control. This encompasses data that comprises sensitive information or data that necessitates segmentation for distinct user groups.
- Establishing Explicit Policies: Develop clear and precise Row Access Policies that describe the specific criteria for filtering. The formulation of these policies may be predicated upon factors such as user roles, department affiliations, or other criteria that are congruent with the access control needs of the system.
- Role-Based Access Control (RBAC) is a method of assigning row access policies to users based on their roles and permissions. By establishing a correlation between rules and roles, it is possible to verify that user access is in accordance with their assigned tasks and permissions.
- Systematic Testing and Validation: It is imperative to conduct comprehensive testing of Row Access Policies in a controlled environment to ascertain their proper functionality. The verification process ensures that users are restricted to accessing only the rows for which they possess authorization.
- The process of auditing and monitoring should be conducted on a regular basis to ensure the proper implementation of Row Access Policies. Snowflake offers auditing capabilities that enable the monitoring of data access and visibility of specific rows, thereby ensuring adherence to data security and privacy standards.

Pitfalls to Avoid

While Row Access Policies are a valuable tool for data security, there are possible problems to be aware of:

- **Overly Complex Policies**: Creating overly complex Row Access Policies might lead to performance difficulties and make policies difficult to monitor. Keep policies as minimal as possible while addressing your security requirements.
- **Inadequate Testing**: Failing to adequately test Row Access Policies before deploying them in a production environment might lead to unintentional data exposure or data that are difficult to deal with.

- **Policy Conflicts**: Carefully monitor and review Row Access Policies to avoid conflicts or unintentional interactions between policies. Conflicting policies can result in unexpected behavior.
- **Neglecting Updates**: As data evolves and access control requirements change, it's vital to update and maintain Row Access Policies properly. Neglecting upgrades can result in data breaches or gaps in protection.

Best Practices for Row Access Policies

In order to optimize the utilization of Row Access Policies in Snowflake and mitigate potential challenges, it is advisable to adhere to the following recommended guidelines:

- It is imperative to remain well-informed regarding the dynamic nature of privacy regulations and to adapt Row Access Policies accordingly in order to maintain compliance.
- Regularly conducting reviews and updates of policies is essential in order to ensure that Row Access Policies remain up-to-date and aligned with evolving data and emerging access control requirements.
- Education and Training: It is imperative to provide comprehensive knowledge and training to users and administrators on Row Access Policies and their associated ramifications. This promotes a climate of data security.
- One approach to enhance data security is through the utilization of data classification, which involves categorizing data according to its level of sensitivity. This enables the implementation of more detailed Row Access Policies, so providing a more refined level of control over data access. Not all data necessitates an equivalent degree of safeguarding.
- Employ Auditing Tools: Utilize the auditing tools provided by Snowflake to properly monitor data access and verify the proper implementation of Row Access Policies.

Snowflake's Row Access Policies offer enterprises a robust mechanism for the implementation of precise data security measures and access control. Organizations can achieve an optimal equilibrium between data safety and usability by acquiring a comprehensive comprehension of the functioning of Row Access Policies, proficiently executing them, evading prevalent challenges, and adhering to established guidelines. Row Access Policies enable enterprises to effectively protect sensitive data, adhere to privacy regulations, and ensure that data access is in accordance with the roles and permissions assigned to authorized individuals. In the contemporary era, characterized by the utmost importance placed on data security and privacy, Row Access Policies emerge as an indispensable element within a comprehensive data management framework on the Snowflake platform.

Combining Row Access Policies and Data Masking in Snowflake

Within the dynamic realm of data management, Snowflake presents a diverse range of functionalities aimed at enhancing both data security and access control. Two notable characteristics, namely Row Access Policies and Data Masking, emerge as crucial tools for protecting sensitive data. When employed in combination, these elements establish a robust safeguard against illegal data intrusion, while simultaneously upholding the principles of data confidentiality and usability. This comprehensive chapter aims to examine the combined utilization of Row Access Policies and Data Masking in Snowflake, highlighting its advantages and limitations.

- The implementation of Row Access Policies and Data Masking in conjunction enables enterprises to develop a comprehensive and multi-faceted strategy for data protection. Row Access Policies serve the purpose of imposing limitations on access to particular rows, so guaranteeing that users are granted visibility solely to the data for which they possess authorization. Data masking serves as a complementary measure by effectively concealing sensitive information within the permissible rows.
- Enhanced Control: Row Access Policies offer businesses the ability to exert meticulous control over data access, enabling them to establish exact criteria governing the authorization of individuals to access certain rows. Data masking provides an extra level of security by concealing critical data, even inside approved rows.
- The importance of data security cannot be overstated, but it is equally imperative for enterprises to prioritize data usability and compliance with privacy requirements. Data masking is a technique employed by businesses to preserve the usability of data while ensuring that only authorized users have access to it. This is achieved by presenting the data in a way that is meaningful to users, but at the same time, obfuscating some elements to protect sensitive information. The maintenance of a delicate equilibrium between security and usability is of utmost importance in ensuring adherence to regulatory frameworks, such as GDPR or HIPAA.

- Enhanced privacy is achieved by the utilization of both Row Access Policies and Data Masking, which effectively safeguard data confidentiality. Individuals who lack appropriate access permissions are not only unable to view rows that are prohibited, but they are also incapable of comprehending sensitive material included within rows that they are authorized to access. This additional measure serves to enhance the protection of data privacy.
- Data segmentation is a common practice employed by organizations to divide data into distinct subsets for various user groups or departments. Row Access Policies enable the segregation of data by employing criteria like as user roles or department affiliations, while Data Masking guarantees the concealment of sensitive data inside these segments.

Restrictions and Considerations

When integrating Row Access Policies with Data Masking, it is important to consider certain limitations and factors in order to ensure comprehensive data security.

- The implementation of both Row Access Policies and Data Masking has the potential to affect query performance. Testing and optimizing these features is crucial in order to avoid any negative impact on query response times.
- The management of both Row Access Policies and Data Masking can provide challenges, particularly in the context of extensive datasets, including multiple policies. It is imperative for organizations to develop explicit policies, delineate roles, and assign tasks in order to properly manage these elements.
- It should be noted that not all data masking strategies exhibit compatibility with Row Access Policies. Organizations ought to select masking techniques that are in accordance with the particular use case and security prerequisites.
- The integration of auditing and monitoring functionalities might enhance the complexity of auditing and monitoring processes. It is recommended that organizations establish auditing mechanisms to monitor data access and verify the accurate implementation of policies.
- It is imperative to ensure that the combined strategy strictly conforms to all pertinent compliance standards. Certain businesses and geographical areas impose stringent mandates pertaining to the protection and confidentiality of data, necessitating compliance with these standards.

Best Practices for Combining Row Access Policies and Data Masking

In order to optimize the utilization of Row Access Policies and Data Masking, businesses are advised to adhere to the following recommended procedures while also taking into account the limitations associated with these practices:

- **Precise Policy Definition:** Establish unambiguous and thoroughly documented Row Access Policies and Data Masking procedures that are in accordance with the data security and privacy objectives of your organization.
- **Systematic Testing**: Conduct comprehensive testing of the integrated methodology within a controlled setting to ascertain its compliance with security and performance criteria.
- **Implementation of Role-Based Access Control**: The utilization of role-based access control is proposed as a means to effectively link Row Access Policies and Data Masking rules with designated roles, thereby enhancing the efficiency of access management processes.
- **Performance Optimization:** Enhance queries and policies to limit potential performance implications, ensuring the preservation of efficient data access.
- **Evaluation of Compliance:** Consistently evaluate the integrated methodology to ascertain adherence to pertinent policies and legislation pertaining to data privacy.
- **Auditing and Monitoring**: Utilize the auditing and monitoring capabilities offered by Snowflake to effectively monitor data access and enforce policy compliance.

Impact on Query Performance

Row Access Policies and Data Masking play a crucial role in ensuring the security of data. However, it is important to acknowledge that their implementation may give rise to some performance-related difficulties.

- The implementation of Row Access Policies frequently necessitates the usage of intricate queries to assess user permissions during runtime, resulting in heightened query complexity. The inclusion of these further conditions has the ability to augment the complexity of the query, which may result in a decrease in performance speed.
- The imposition of Row Access Policies introduces filtering constraints that impose additional overhead on the execution of queries. The

performance is directly influenced by the level of complexity in the filtering conditions.

- The process of Data Masking involves performing calculations to convert sensitive data into masked values. The inclusion of these calculations may result in an increase in processing overhead, which might have an impact on the response times of queries.
- Policy evaluation involves the assessment of Row Access Policies by Snowflake for every query, with the aim of deciding the visibility of specific rows for the user. The review process, particularly when complicated policies are involved, may lead to a deceleration of query execution.
- The utilization of resources: The execution of intensive queries arising from Row Access Policies or Data Masking can consume substantial computational resources, hence impacting the overall performance of the Snowflake platform.

Trade-Offs: Balancing Security and Performance

Organizations frequently encounter a dilemma concerning the balance between data security and query efficiency during the implementation of Row Access Policies and Data Masking.

- One potential strategy for mitigating the impact on performance is for organizations to optimize their Row Access Policies and Data Masking implementations in order to minimize any negative effects on system performance. This process may entail the refinement of policy logic, the utilization of more effective masking methods, and the enhancement of query optimization techniques.
- Placing Emphasis on Security: In situations when the utmost importance is given to safeguarding data, businesses may be willing to tolerate a certain level of decline in query performance in exchange for improved data security. This holds particular significance in sectors characterized by rigorous regulatory standards, such as the healthcare and banking industries.
- Role-Based Access Control (RBAC) is a method of organizing roles and permissions in a manner that effectively addresses the potential performance effects. Organizations can mitigate the impact on overall system performance by implementing controls exclusively for users who require them.
- Monitoring and adjusting are essential practices in maintaining optimal query performance and achieving a harmonious equilibrium. Optimizing

the system can be achieved by identifying performance bottlenecks and subsequently modifying policies.

- Resource Scaling: In situations where the impact on performance becomes substantial, businesses have the option to scale Snowflake resources by increasing the size of the warehouse or concurrency, in order to effectively manage the increased computational demand.
- Utilizing the query optimization tools of Snowflake can effectively mitigate the performance repercussions. Query profiling, query caching, and materialized views are notable features that have the potential to improve the efficiency of query execution.
- Data segmentation involves dividing data into different segments based on their sensitivity levels. By implementing row access policies and selectively applying data masking techniques, performance concerns can be alleviated. The allocation of resources inside companies can be optimized by recognizing that different types of data may not necessitate identical levels of security.

Row access policies and data masking are essential mechanisms for enhancing data security and privacy within the Snowflake platform. Nevertheless, it is imperative for enterprises to recognize that the implementation of these security measures may have adverse effects on the performance of queries. The trade-offs pertaining to security and performance exhibit variability contingent upon an organization's aims, industry affiliation, and regulatory framework.

Achieving an optimal equilibrium between security and performance is an ongoing endeavor that encompasses the refinement of policies, efficient allocation of resources, and meticulous evaluation of individual usage scenarios. Although there is a legitimate concern regarding the impact on performance, firms should not be discouraged from implementing comprehensive data security measures. This is particularly crucial at a time when the occurrence of data breaches and privacy violations is more worrisome.

In order to make sound decisions, companies must consider their distinct security and performance needs, acknowledging that attaining an ideal balance between the two may not always be attainable. The crucial aspect lies in the ongoing evaluation and adjustment of security protocols in response to the changing requirements of data management, all the while ensuring a satisfactory degree of operational efficiency.

Business Use Case

Let's explore a practical example in the world of business where Snowflake's masking procedures can be utilized to safeguard sensitive data, such as credit card information, in real-time. The financial services organization has implemented a consolidated analytics dashboard specifically designed for executives and managers to closely monitor key performance indicators (KPIs) pertaining to client interactions, revenue, and overall financial performance. Nevertheless, the dashboard must exhibit credit card information in an obscured fashion to adhere to data privacy standards and safeguard delicate customer particulars.

To begin, we must first identify the sensitive data, which in this case is the credit card number. Credit card information is considered sensitive and necessitates safeguarding. We can proceed by implementing the following measures to protect this data.

Snowflake Masking Policy:

1. Create a masking policy in Snowflake specifically for credit card information.

Define the masking logic to replace all but the last four digits of the credit card numbers with asterisks.

```
CREATE MASKING POLICY credit_card_masking_policy ADD COLUMN cred-
it_card COLUMN_POLICY ('FULL_MASKING');
```

Applying Masking Policy to a Table:

2. Apply the masking policy to the table containing the credit card information.

```
ALTER TABLE financial_transactions MODIFY COLUMN credit_card SET
MASKING POLICY credit_card_masking_policy;
```

Dashboard Integration:

1. Integrate the masked credit card data into the financial reporting dashboard.
2. Ensure that only users with the appropriate access privileges can view the unmasked data.

Role-Based Access Control (RBAC):

1. Implement RBAC in Snowflake to control access to the financial transactions table.
2. Define roles (for example, Executive, Manager) and assign appropriate privileges to each role.

3. Grant the necessary **SELECT** privilege on the masked credit card column only to users with the Executive role.

   ```
   GRANT SELECT (credit_card) ON TABLE financial_transactions TO ROLE
   Executive;
   ```

Executives and managers have the ability to access the financial reporting dashboard and see significant metrics, such as credit card details. The credit card numbers are automatically obfuscated in accordance with the specified policy, revealing just the final four digits. Access controls guarantee that only authorized users possessing the Executive position can access and read the unmasked data. The method guarantees adherence to data privacy standards by obfuscating sensitive information. Exclusive individuals with proper authorization possess the ability to retrieve the complete payment card information. Executives and managers can utilize masked data to make well-informed decisions while maintaining security. By utilizing Snowflake's masking policies alongside RBAC, enterprises may achieve a harmonious equilibrium between data accessibility and security, guaranteeing the sufficient safeguarding of critical information while yet enabling valuable insights for decision-making.

Conclusion

This chapter on Snowflake Row Access Policies and Data Masking sheds light on two key data security and privacy issues in the Snowflake data warehousing technology. Row Access Policies and Data Masking help enterprises balance data security and query performance.

Row-Level Security (RLS) allows enterprises to limit data access via Row Access Policies. This feature restricts data rows to authorized users or roles based on predefined criteria. These concepts help organizations comply with data security and compliance laws and segment data efficiently.

Data masking protects sensitive data by concealing it. Businesses can use masked values to replace sensitive data with veiled values, allowing authorized users to operate with the data while unauthorized users see hidden information. Data masking protects sensitive data like PII and financial records while preserving its usefulness.

In this chapter, these pros and cons were examined. Row Access Policies and Data Masking improve data security, privacy, and compliance, which are crucial in a data-driven world. These solutions help organizations comply with GDPR, HIPAA, and other regulations while protecting sensitive company data.

The next chapter will reveal Snowflake's unique tagging system's unmatched data security. Tag sensitive data for granular control and visibility to improve cloud data safety. Tag-based access policies make it easy to restrict data access to authorized users. Snowflake's dynamic tagging adapts to changing security needs, preventing unauthorized access and breaches. Snowflake's tag-driven security protects your data with precision and efficiency, setting new cloud-based security standards. Snowflake's cutting-edge tagging technology offers a future where data safety and flexibility coexist.

CHAPTER 6

Snowflake Security Framework

Introduction

The primary objective of the Snowflake security architecture is to offer enterprises a comprehensive and resilient approach to protecting their data assets. Snowflake's security features and capabilities effectively safeguard data confidentiality, integrity, and availability, thereby enabling enterprises to construct a secure and reliable data environment.

Snowflake Tags serve as the fundamental building blocks of Snowflake's security mechanism. Snowflake Tags refer to metadata IDs that are capable of being allocated to various objects inside the Snowflake data platform, such as tables, columns, and views. These IDs provide a versatile and scalable approach to categorizing and structuring data based on several factors, including the sensitivity of the data, regulatory obligations, and organizational units.

The utilization of identifiers in data classification facilitates the implementation of precise access restrictions and security rules inside enterprises. By assigning tags to data items, organizations can effectively establish and enforce access restrictions and data management principles. For example, administrators might apply labels such as "*Confidential*" or "*PII*" to sensitive data, enabling the implementation of more stringent access controls and supplementary security measures to protect the data.

The security framework of Snowflake encompasses more than just the use of tags for data classification. Furthermore, it encompasses other components such as data encryption, authentication systems, role-based access control, and auditing features. These functionalities guarantee the safeguarding of data in both stationary and moving states, the regulation and surveillance of user access, and the recording of all platform operations for the sake of compliance and security.

Through the utilization of Snowflake's security architecture, enterprises have the ability to develop a strong security stance, protect valuable data assets, and ensure adherence to regulatory obligations. The implementation of Snowflake Tags for the purpose of data classification enhances data management practices and facilitates the establishment of access controls that are aligned with the sensitivity of the data and the specific requirements of the company.

Structure

In this chapter, we will cover the following topics:

- Snowflake Tag
- Data Classification Using Tag
- Other Security Features

Snowflake Tags Enhance Data Management

Within the domain of cloud data warehousing, Snowflake has positioned itself as a multifaceted platform that provides an extensive range of functionalities to enhance the efficiency of data organization and administration. Among the several capabilities available, Snowflake Tags are particularly notable for their ability to significantly improve data classification, resource management, and governance. This paper examines the effective utilization of Snowflake Tags and presents recommended strategies for maximizing their capabilities within the context of a data catalog.

Understanding Snowflake Tags

Snowflake Tags are personalized designations or metadata that users have the ability to allocate to various Snowflake entities, including databases, schemas, tables, views, and even specific columns. The aforementioned tags serve as descriptive labels or attributes, allowing users to efficiently categorize, classify, and organize their data and resources in a way that corresponds with their company's structure and objectives.

Tags can be defined as pairs consisting of a key and a corresponding value. Each tag consists of a label, which functions as the primary identifier, and a value, which denotes the material associated with the tag. One way to demonstrate this is by creating a tag labeled **`"Department"`** and assigning it the value **`"Marketing"`** to indicate the association of a certain table with the marketing department. A Snowflake object has the capability to be assigned many tags, which enhance the flexibility in the organization and administration of resources.

Effective Use Cases for Snowflake Tags

- Categorization of Resources: Tags can be employed to categorize various Snowflake objects, including databases, schemas, tables, and others, by utilizing qualities such as department, project, data sensitivity, or data source. The act of categorizing streamlines the process of discovering and managing resources.
- Cost Allocation: Organizations have the ability to utilize tags in order to enhance the efficiency of cost allocation. For example, the utilization of tags facilitates the allocation of expenses to particular business units or projects, hence enhancing financial transparency and optimizing resource management.
- Data governance is enhanced by the use of tags, as they enable the labeling of data assets with metadata pertaining to data lineage, data owners, compliance statuses, and data classification, such as personally identifiable information (PII), sensitive data, and public data.
- Environmental Management: Labels can serve as indicators of the specific environment in which an object is utilized, encompassing categories such as **`"Development", "Testing"`**, or **`"Production".`** This practice guarantees that both users and administrators possess knowledge regarding the specific circumstances in which a resource is implemented.
- Security and Access Control: Tags can be utilized to contribute to access control mechanisms by facilitating the identification of data sensitivity, such as categorizing it as **`"Confidential"`** or **`"Public",`** and subsequently implementing suitable security rules.

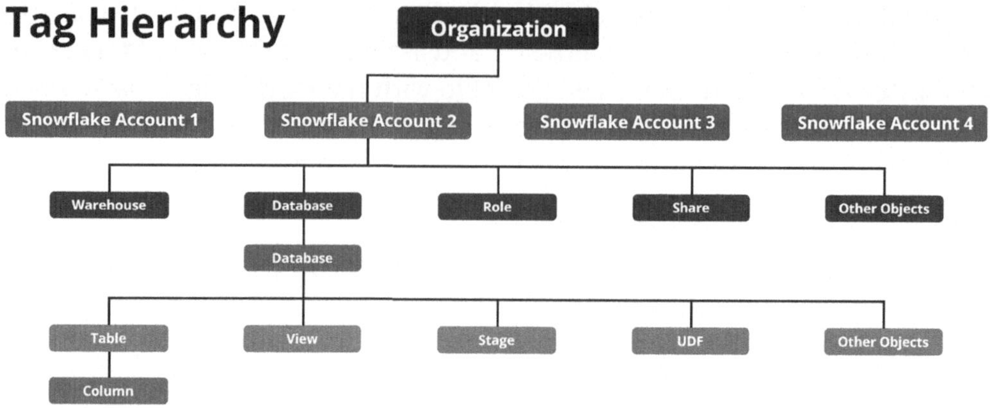

***Figure 6.1**: Snowflake Tag Hierarchy*

Best Practices for Snowflake Tags

In order to optimize the utilization of Snowflake Tags and ensure effective organization and management of data, it is advisable to adhere to the following recommended practices:

- **Develop a Tagging Strategy**: Prior to applying tags, it is imperative to have a well-defined tagging strategy that is congruent with the objectives of the company. The establishment of a set of standardized labels (keys) and values is necessary in order to ensure consistent categorization of resources.
- **Ensuring Uniform Tagging Practices Amongst Teams**: Promote the adoption of uniform tagging protocols throughout various teams and departments. The implementation of standardized tag usage guarantees that all users can efficiently explore the data catalog.
- **Utilize Hierarchies**: One might employ hierarchical tags in order to establish organized taxonomies. An example of a hierarchical structure that can be implemented is one that includes levels such as `"Department,"` `"Project,"` and `"Data Sensitivity,"` thus enabling a more refined categorization of resources.
- **Conventions for Document Tagging**: Please provide comprehensive documentation of your tagging conventions, ensuring that it is easily available to all users and administrators. The purpose of this documentation is to provide a comprehensive explanation of the significance and application of each tag.
- **Implement Automation for Tagging When Applicable**: Employ automation techniques to streamline the tagging process whenever it is

practicable. The utilization of tools and scripts can effectively optimize the process of tagging by implementing predetermined criteria, hence minimizing the need for manual labor and mitigating the potential for inaccuracies.

- **Regular Audits and Maintenance**: It is advisable to consistently examine and update tags in order to ensure their ongoing relevance. The evolution of data, initiatives, and resources necessitates corresponding updates to their tags in order to accurately reflect these changes.
- **Training of Users and Administrators**: Offer comprehensive training and assistance to both users and administrators regarding the proficient utilization and accurate interpretation of tags. This educational program ensures that tags are effectively employed to maximize their potential.
- **Monitoring of Tag Usage**: One important aspect to consider is the monitoring of tag usage. It is advisable to closely monitor the practical application of tags. It is also advisable to conduct periodic evaluations of tagged resources in order to ascertain their conformity with the established tagging strategy and conventions.

Snowflake Tags provide a multifaceted and indispensable method for organizing, categorizing, and effectively managing data and resources within the Snowflake platform. Organizations can get several benefits by proficiently utilizing tags, including the streamlining of data cataloging processes, enhancement of resource management practices, optimization of cost allocation strategies, reinforcement of data governance measures, and improvement of overall data organization.

In order to fully leverage the capabilities of Snowflake Tags, it is imperative for enterprises to develop a well-defined tagging strategy, encourage uniformity across different teams, and implement automated tagging procedures whenever feasible. Regular evaluations and revisions of tags, in conjunction with user education, are vital to uphold the currency and efficacy of tags within a dynamic data setting.

Snowflake Tags serve as a valuable resource within the realm of data management, augmenting one's capacity to effectively navigate and oversee data inside the dynamic domain of cloud-based data warehousing. When tags are employed strategically and in accordance with established principles, they enable enterprises to enhance their operational effectiveness, ensure compliance, and exercise authority over their data assets within the Snowflake platform.

Tags for Data Categorization

In the modern data-driven landscape, effective data management is paramount. Understanding and categorizing data is a foundational step in this process.

Snowflake's data catalog offers a robust feature for data classification using tags. In this chapter, we will explore how data classification tags can be employed and highlight best practices for implementing this feature in Snowflake's data catalog.

Data classification tags are labels or metadata attributes that can be assigned to databases, tables, or even individual columns within Snowflake's data catalog. These tags provide valuable information about the nature, purpose, and sensitivity of data, aiding in its organization, searchability, and management.

In Snowflake, tags can be added to databases, tables, or columns using SQL statements or through the Snowflake web interface. Tags are user-defined, allowing organizations to create a taxonomy that aligns with their specific needs. Users can then search for tagged data, helping them find relevant information quickly.

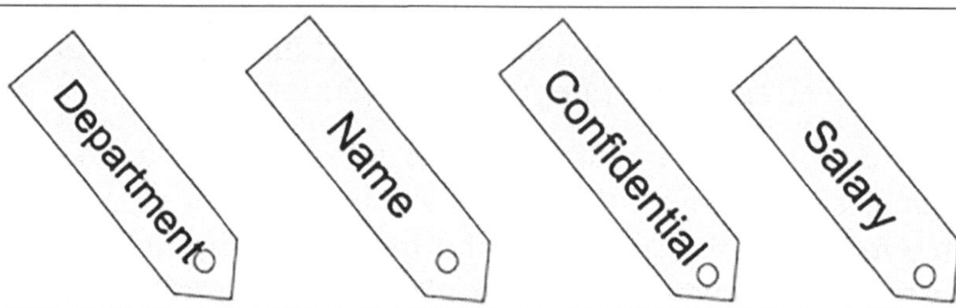

Employee ID	Dept	Emp Nm	Emp Tax ID	Compensation
1345	HR	Ann Susan	145674398	$78,964
5678	Finance	Ram Prakash	345654409	$48,984
10011	R&D	Nandini	545634420	$36,004
14344	HR	Meenakshi	745614431	$44,691
18677	Tech	Sam Baker	945594442	$38,933

Figure 6.2: *Snowflake Tag for Data Classification Hierarchy*

Use Cases for Data Classification Tags

- The utilization of tags can serve as an effective means to denote the sensitivity of data, facilitating organizational adherence to privacy standards such as the General Data Protection Regulation (GDPR) or the Health Insurance Portability and Accountability Act (HIPAA). For example, the act of labeling data as "PII" (Personally Identifiable Information) or "Confidential" serves to guarantee that users treat the information in a suitable manner.

- Ownership and Stewardship of Data: Tags have the capability to designate the individuals or entities who possess the rights and responsibilities for overseeing and preserving particular datasets. This facilitates the optimization of data governance and enhances accountability.
- Utilization and Significance of Data: Tags have the capability to delineate the intended application or objective of data. An illustrative instance is the use of tags such as **`"Sales"`** or **`"Marketing"`** which facilitates users in promptly discerning material that is pertinent to their respective department.
- The Significance of Tags in Assessing Data Quality Levels: For example, data can be categorized as either **`"Verified"`** or **`"Needs Review,"`** facilitating endeavors in data quality control.
- The Data lifespan: Tags can be used to indicate the current stage of data within its lifespan. Tags such as "Production" or "Archived" serve the purpose of providing users with a clear understanding of the current status of the data.

Best Practices for Data Classification using Tags:

- **Provide a Precise Definition of a Tag Taxonomy**: Develop a well-defined and all-encompassing categorization system for tags that is in accordance with the specific requirements of your organization. It is advisable to engage in dialogues with important parties involved in order to ascertain the most pertinent tags.
- **Maintaining Consistency**: The importance of maintaining consistency in achieving success. It is important to ensure uniformity in the application of tags. It is imperative to enforce adherence to established naming rules and discourage the use of duplicate or redundant tags among users.
- **Data Stewardship:** The allocation of tagging responsibilities to data stewards or owners is recommended. These professionals should possess a comprehensive understanding of the properties and utilization of the data, hence enabling them to assign appropriate tags to it.
- **Training and Education**: Offer training sessions and educational materials to users with the aim of fostering comprehension of the tagging system and its associated advantages. The likelihood of data classification being embraced is higher when the user community is well-informed.
- **Regular Evaluation and Upkeep**: Conduct periodic assessments and make necessary revisions to tags in order to maintain their accuracy and relevance. The classification of data should be updated as it undergoes evolution.

- **Incorporation of Data Governance**: Effectuates the integration of data classification tags into the overarching data governance architecture. It is advisable to integrate these practices and processes with other data management strategies.
- **Utilize Automation**: It is advisable to employ automation tools or scripts to reliably and efficiently apply tags in a large-scale manner. The implementation of automation can contribute to the preservation of tag correctness and completeness.
- **Implementation of Tagging Policies**: It is advisable to implement tagging policies by means of role-based access controls (RBAC) or other governance mechanisms. This technique guarantees that tagging is not discretionary, but rather a customary procedure.
- **Establishment of Document Tag Definitions**: Develop a comprehensive library of documentation that enables users to readily access tag definitions and guidelines. The availability of this documentation is crucial in facilitating users' comprehension of the significance and intent behind each tag.

Benefits of Data Classification Tags

The implementation of tags facilitates the process of users locating and retrieving pertinent material. Users have the ability to efficiently apply filters and conduct searches to locate datasets according to their assigned tags. Enhanced data governance is achieved through the utilization of data classification tags, which serve as a crucial element in ensuring the effectiveness of data governance practices. These professionals assist firms in effectively managing and preserving data while ensuring its utilization aligns with regulatory requirements and industry standards.

The utilization of tags facilitates the process of data administration by offering contextual details and informative attributes pertaining to datasets. The utilization of this approach facilitates the organization of data, management of quality, and the process of decision-making. The utilization of tags facilitates collaboration among users by streamlining the process of locating and exchanging data. Efficiency in team collaboration can be enhanced by the ability to promptly seek and retrieve necessary data. The adaptability and scalability of data classification tags enable enterprises to adjust and expand their data management strategies in response to changes in their data ecosystem.

The utilization of tags in Snowflake's data catalog for data classification is a robust mechanism that effectively augments the administration, governance, and exploration of data. Organizations can optimize the utilization of these tags through the implementation of best practices, resulting in improved efficiency in data management, strengthened data governance, and increased discoverability and accessibility of data. When data classification tags are implemented with careful consideration, they become a highly important asset in the contemporary data-driven society. They play a crucial role in ensuring that data is not only viewed as an asset but also as a resource that is well-organized and managed.

Snowflake's Alert Feature: Tag-Based Data Management Improvements

Snowflake innovates data operations tools for enterprises. Snowflake's new alert function, along with data classification tags, helps enterprises design data monitoring, management, and governance processes. This section will cover Snowflake's alert function, its use with tags, and how it can streamline data operations.

The inclusion of Snowflake's introduced alert capability is an integral component of the overarching Snowflake Data Cloud platform. The Snowflake platform enables businesses to establish personalized alerts that are activated by certain events or situations. The warnings can be derived from a diverse set of characteristics, encompassing query performance, resource use, data modifications, and security breaches.

The alert function provided by Snowflake enables users to establish specific criteria and thresholds for triggering alerts. Alerts are triggered by the system when the predefined conditions are met or surpassed. These notifications can be disseminated through several communication methods, including email, SMS, or integration with external software, ensuring timely dissemination of crucial information to pertinent individuals involved.

Leveraging Data Classification Tags for Alerting

The alert functionality of Snowflake can be greatly improved with the utilization of data classification tags. Organizations have the ability to establish tag-based procedures that automate alerting based on data qualities by linking tags to specific data assets.

Organizations can establish alert systems by assigning sensitivity levels (such as "`Confidential,`" "`Sensitive,`" or "`Public`") to tagged data, enabling the detection of unauthorized access, modification, or sharing of sensitive information. This measure guarantees prompt response to potential security breaches or violations of compliance. Tags can be employed for the purpose of categorizing degrees of data quality, such as **"Verified," "Incomplete,"** and **"Requires Review"**. Alerts can be designed to activate in instances where data quality diminishes or when specific data validation rules are breached, thus facilitating proactive control of data quality.

Tags can serve as indicators of the intended use of data, such as **"Sales", "Finance",** or **"HR"**. Organizations have the capability to establish warning systems in order to monitor instances of unanticipated or unauthorized data access outside its permitted scope, guaranteeing that data is employed solely for its intended purpose. The utilization of tags to assign data owners or stewards enables businesses to develop alert mechanisms for changes in ownership or data stewardship duties. This measure guarantees that data is consistently maintained under responsible management throughout its whole.

Tags can be used to indicate the current stage of data throughout its lifespan, such as **"Production"** or **"Archived".** Organizations have the capability to establish alarm systems that are activated when data is accessed or modified at particular phases of its lifespan. This feature assists in upholding data governance and ensuring compliance with relevant regulations.

Creating Well-Defined Processes with Alerting and Tags

Establish concrete standards for when warnings should be generated. The first step is to determine whether circumstances or events require attention, such as data breaches, poor data quality, or illegal access.

Make sure your company's data management goals are reflected in the taxonomy of tags you develop. Verify that the tags you use adequately describe the sensitivity, ownership, purpose, quality, and lifetime of your data.

Tag information systematically depending on the attributes of the information's assets. Consistently and precisely tagging data is essential for automated alerting procedures to function. Set up notifications based on tag attributes using Snowflake's built-in alerting features. Define alerting thresholds and notification channels, defining who should be informed when specified conditions are satisfied.

Make sure the systems you have in place for alerting based on tags have been thoroughly tested. To reduce the number of false positives and maximize response times, it is important to fine-tune the criteria and thresholds used for alerting.

Tag-based alerting should be incorporated into your larger data governance system. Align alerts with governance policies to make it easier to follow rules and regulations, both external and internal.

Always keep an eye on data properties and set up real-time notifications with continuous monitoring. In order to keep up with the ever-evolving needs of data management, it is important to regularly examine and update tag-based systems.

Benefits of Combining Alerting and Tags

The integration of alerting and tags enables enterprises to adopt a proactive stance towards data management. Instead of adopting a reactive approach towards difficulties, firms have the ability to swiftly respond to anticipated problems, thereby reducing risks and streamlining data operations.

The implementation of automated warning systems that rely on tags enhances the effectiveness of data governance initiatives. The implementation of this system guarantees the consistent management, classification, and protection of data in accordance with predetermined criteria, hence easing adherence to data privacy rules and industry standards.

Tag-based alerts have the capability to promptly detect and resolve data quality concerns in real-time. As a consequence, there is an increase in the levels of data quality and greater reliability in decision-making that is driven by data. The use of clearly defined tag-based processes facilitates enhanced collaboration among individuals responsible for managing and utilizing data. Alerts play a crucial role in facilitating timely communication to relevant parties, hence enabling coordinated actions in reaction to data-related occurrences.

Through the implementation of automated alerting mechanisms, companies have the potential to mitigate operational expenses that arise from the need for manual monitoring and intervention. The aforementioned efficiency leads to long-term cost reductions.

Utilizing Snowflake tags in the healthcare sector can greatly improve adherence to legal mandates like HIPAA and safeguard confidential patient data, hence bolstering data security.

As an illustration, a healthcare institution that stores patient data in Snowflake can employ tags to classify data according to its level of sensitivity, such as patient demographics, medical history, or treatment records. Every category can be allocated a distinct tag, denoting the amount of access control and security measures needed.

Snowflake tags enable administrators to enforce precise access controls by assigning distinct roles or permissions to each tag. Authorized medical professionals with the necessary credentials are the only ones allowed to see patient treatment records, while administrative personnel may only be able to examine patient demographics.

In addition, Snowflake tags allow enterprises to more efficiently enforce data retention regulations. Organizations can mitigate the risk of unwanted access or data breaches by assigning expiration dates or retention periods to data, which enables automated archiving or deletion of data once it reaches the end of its lifecycle.

In addition, Snowflake tags enhance auditing and compliance endeavors by offering insight into data access and usage according to tag categories. Organizations can monitor the individuals who have accessed confidential information, together with the specific time and reason for access, thereby assuring responsibility and adherence to regulations.

Utilizing Snowflake tags in the healthcare sector allows enterprises to establish precise access controls, enforce data preservation policies, and strengthen auditing and compliance capabilities, thereby enhancing data security. Organizations can effectively reduce the likelihood of data breaches, safeguard patient privacy, and ensure compliance with regulations by classifying and labeling data according to its level of sensitivity.

Security Features of Snowflake

Snowflake provides a wide range of security measures to protect data and resources, including multi-factor authentication (MFA), network policies, single sign-on (SSO), and secured views.

Multi-Factor Authentication (MFA) is a security feature supported by Snowflake. It enhances security by demanding users to prove their identity through various authentication methods. This measure serves to prevent unauthorized access, hence reducing the likelihood of credential theft or misuse.

Snowflake has the capability for administrators to establish network policies that regulate access to the Snowflake service by specifying IP address ranges or Virtual Private Cloud (VPC) peering. This feature guarantees that only approved networks are able to establish a connection with Snowflake, hence minimizing the potential points of attack and enhancing the overall security of the network.

A Single Sign-On (SSO) connection with Snowflake allows users to authenticate using their current identity provider (IdP) credentials, simplifying the authentication procedure and improving user experience. Single Sign-On (SSO) streamlines access management by consolidating it in one place, making it easier to manage user provisioning and deprovisioning across many platforms.

Snowflake's secured views feature enables administrators to establish precise access controls at the row and column level, limiting access to sensitive data according to user roles and permissions. This guarantees that users are only granted access to the data they have been allowed to view, hence reducing the likelihood of data breaches or illegal data access.

By utilizing these security capabilities, enterprises may implement strong security measures within Snowflake, safeguarding sensitive data, and guaranteeing compliance with legal mandates. By implementing Multi-Factor Authentication (MFA), network policies, Single Sign-On (SSO), and secured views, the entire security of Snowflake deployments is reinforced. This helps to reduce security risks and improve the ability to protect data.

Conclusion

This chapter on Snowflake security framework has shown how important this functionality is in modern data management and governance. Snowflake's Data Cloud relies on tags to organize, categorize, and secure data. They help preserve data quality, security, and compliance by improving data discoverability and governance.

We have covered Snowflake tags' generation, application, and best practices in this chapter. Following these recommended practices and using tags, enterprises may maximize their Snowflake data environment.

Tags are customizable to an organization's needs. Snowflake tags standardize data management by classifying data by sensitivity, ownership, intended use, and lifecycle stage.

Tags' integration with Snowflake's other capabilities, such as alerting, allows for inventive data management. Tagging alerts can automate key data event reactions, informing the right people quickly, lowering risks, and streamlining data operations. Tags support data stewardship in a data-driven world where fast decisions depend on data accuracy and availability. They streamline procedures, improve stakeholder communication, and enable data-driven excellence.

Snowflake tags underpin efficient data governance as firms exploit data's power. They manage and govern data to boost business development, innovation, and resilience. Overall, Snowflake tags represent a template for better data management, not merely labels. Organizations can navigate new data environments and keep data an asset by adopting and using tags. Such preparation prepares them for the data-centric world of today and the future.

Our following chapter will show how Snowflake deployment requires careful consideration of varied organizational elements to achieve peak performance. From data architecture alignment to user training protocols, this comprehensive chapter covers implementation details. Consider cost-effective and scalable performance optimization strategies. Discover best practices for seamless system integration to create a harmonious tech ecosystem. The chapter helps businesses unleash the full potential of Snowflake, helping them toward a successful deployment that meets their unique needs and goals.

CHAPTER 7

Deployment Considerations

Introduction

Organizations must consider many variables while installing Snowflake to guarantee optimal performance and a successful installation. Deployment considerations include selecting the right Snowflake region, handling data management needs, and creating a strong disaster recovery plan.

Performance, compliance, and data ownership are all significantly impacted by selecting the appropriate Snowflake region. Businesses can choose from a variety of Snowflake locations around the world to decrease data latency and meet their data residency requirements. This choice should take into account things like user accessibility, legal compliance, and operational needs.

For Snowflake to maintain data security, integrity, and governance, data management considerations are crucial. Data management procedures, such as workflows for data ingestion, transformation, and integration, must be established by organizations. They must also provide data governance standards, data retention regulations, and data quality monitoring systems to guarantee data accuracy and consistency.

A crucial component of any data platform is business continuity, which is ensured by the strong processes offered by Snowflake. Organizations should put in place a disaster recovery plan that includes routine backups, replication across regions, and failover protocols to reduce data loss and disruption in the event of a disaster.

By carefully weighing deployment choices, addressing data management issues, and putting in place a strong disaster recovery plan, organizations may guarantee a successful and resilient Snowflake implementation. These factors are crucial for maintaining high data availability, guaranteeing data integrity, and maximizing Snowflake's effectiveness.

Effective data management is a fundamental aspect of every thriving firm that relies on data-driven decision-making. Snowflake, a prominent data warehousing platform, provides a comprehensive environment for the effective management, storage, and analysis of data. This comprehensive chapter aims to examine crucial data management aspects in Snowflake, with the intention of assisting enterprises in making well-informed decisions and optimizing the value derived from their data assets.

Structure

In this chapter, the following topics to be covered:

- Data Management Considerations
- Choice of Snowflake Region
- Disaster Recovery

Data Ingestion and Integration

Data sources are vital to contemplate the diverse array of data sources upon which one's corporation depends. Snowflake facilitates the integration of data from various sources, encompassing databases, data lakes, and external systems. Assess the extent to which Snowflake can effectively accept source types that are peculiar to your requirements.

Snowflake offers a range of integration tools, including Snowpipe and Stream which facilitate the process of data import. Evaluate the appropriateness of these solutions for your data ingestion needs, taking into consideration factors such as data volume, frequency, and complexity.

Data preprocessing is the necessity of preprocessing or transforming your data prior to storage. The alignment between Snowflake's capabilities for ETL operations and data transformations should be assessed to the specific requirements of your data transformation needs.

The Snowflake Data Marketplace is a popular data source that is highly regarded for its ability to expedite, simplify, safeguard, and cost-efficiently enable the interchange of data.

Data Modeling and Organization

The selection of a suitable data modeling approach is crucial in ensuring alignment with one's data analytics and reporting requirements. Snowflake supports star schema, snowflake schema, and raw data vault. Choose the most appropriate technique depending on the specific needs and demands of your organization.

The precise preparation of schema design is crucial in the process of schema design. Utilize the adaptable nature of Snowflake to design schemas that enhance query efficiency and adapt to dynamic changes in data structures.

The Data Catalog leverages the inherent data catalog functionality provided by Snowflake to document and arrange metadata. The utilization of tags, descriptions, and comments has the potential to improve the discoverability and control of data.

Data Security and Access Control

The implementation of fine-grained access restrictions can be achieved by utilizing Snowflake's Role-Based Access Control (RBAC) system. To ensure appropriate access to data, it is imperative to establish clear definitions and delineations of roles, permissions, and privileges for users. This entails assigning specific responsibilities and authorizations to individuals based on their respective needs and requirements. By implementing such measures, organizations may effectively restrict data access to just those who require it, thereby enhancing data security and minimizing potential risks.

It is imperative to give precedence to the implementation of data encryption measures both during data storage and data transmission. Snowflake offers a comprehensive range of encryption solutions, enabling users to effectively protect and secure critical data.

The implementation of data masking measures is necessary to safeguard sensitive data. The Data Masking function offered by Snowflake facilitates the implementation of dynamic masking techniques to safeguard sensitive information, hence assuring the preservation of data privacy and compliance with relevant regulations.

The Snowflake Tri-Secret Encryption system guarantees robust data security through the integration of customer-managed keys, service-managed keys, and account master key encryption layers. In addition, Snowflake offers external tokenization as a means to tokenize sensitive data, improving data protection and ensuring compliance with privacy standards.

Data Governance and Compliance

To provide comprehensive oversight of data access, modifications, and user behavior, it is recommended to activate the auditing and monitoring functionalities inside the Snowflake platform. This practice guarantees adherence to regulatory mandates and improves the management of data.

Data retention policies refer to the established guidelines and procedures implemented by organizations to effectively manage the lifespan of data. These policies outline the specific time for which data should be retained, as well as the methods and processes for its storage, archiving, and eventual disposal. By adhering to data retention policies, organizations can ensure compliance with legal and regulatory requirements, and mitigate risks associated. The Time-Travel and Data Archival functionalities of Snowflake contribute to the preservation of historical data while simultaneously optimizing storage expenses.

Evaluate the extent to which Snowflake conforms to the compliance guidelines relevant to your industry. Snowflake adheres to multiple regulatory standards, namely the General Data Protection Regulation (GDPR), the Health Insurance Portability and Accountability Act (HIPAA), and the Service Organization Control 2 (SOC 2).

Data Quality Management

Incorporate data validation mechanisms to ascertain the precision and reliability of the data. Snowflake facilitates the monitoring and certification of data quality by offering support for SQL queries and external tools.

To swiftly address data quality issues, it is imperative to establish error-handling systems. The data transformation capabilities of Snowflake can be utilized to facilitate the identification and rectification of errors.

Scalability and Performance

It is important to consider the degree to which Snowflake's elastic scalability capabilities can effectively handle fluctuations in query and data processing requirements. This section delineates a strategic framework for resource allocation and the execution of scaling methods with the aim of optimizing performance and minimizing expenses.

Utilize Snowflake's query profiling and optimization functionalities to identify and rectify performance problems. It is recommended to integrate indexing and materialized views in instances where they are considered beneficial.

Data Backup and Disaster Recovery

The task at hand involves the formulation of a comprehensive and resilient backup and disaster recovery plan. The Time-Travel and Fail-Safe functionalities of Snowflake provide the retrieval of data at certain points in time and guarantee the uninterrupted operation of business processes.

The implementation of data replication is essential to achieve both redundancy and availability. Snowflake facilitates the replication of data across several regions to augment the robustness of data.

Snowflake's data archival technique incorporates the capacity to efficiently store historical data, hence minimizing storage expenses while ensuring continued accessibility. Snowflake ensures data loss prevention and secure management and retention of vital information by using rigorous deletion procedures. The integration of efficient archival procedures and strict deletion controls offers a thorough strategy for managing the lifecycle of data within the Snowflake platform.

Snowflake employs a multi-cluster, multi-availability zone architecture to improve the availability and resilience of data. Data is duplicated across various Availability Zones within a chosen region. If there is a breakdown in one Availability Zone or even a whole data center, the data will still be accessible from other duplicated copies, guaranteeing the uninterrupted provision of services.

Cost Management

It is imperative to closely monitor and analyze the utilization and expenditures associated with Snowflake. Leverage the cost management capabilities offered by Snowflake, such as the Snowflake Cost Explorer, to enhance expenditure optimization.

It is advisable to engage in regular assessments and enhancements of resource utilization in order to prevent over-provisioning and minimize expenses.

The successful management of data in Snowflake involves various aspects, including data integration, modeling, security, governance, quality, performance, and cost management. By taking into account these crucial factors, firms may effectively utilize the complete range of possibilities offered by Snowflake, guaranteeing that data retains its status as a strategic asset that propels business insights and fosters innovation.

The administration of data in Snowflake is a continuous and dynamic process that adapts to the evolving data requirements of a company, rather than being a one-time undertaking. By maintaining a state of constant awareness, adjusting to evolving data environments, and efficiently utilizing the capabilities of Snowflake, individuals can successfully negotiate the intricacies of contemporary data management and excel within the context of a data-centric environment.

Choose the Best Snowflake Region for your Account

Your data warehousing performance, latency, and data residency compliance depend on the Snowflake region you choose. Snowflake has many regions with different cloud providers, each with benefits. This section will cover important variables to consider while picking the right Snowflake area for your purposes.

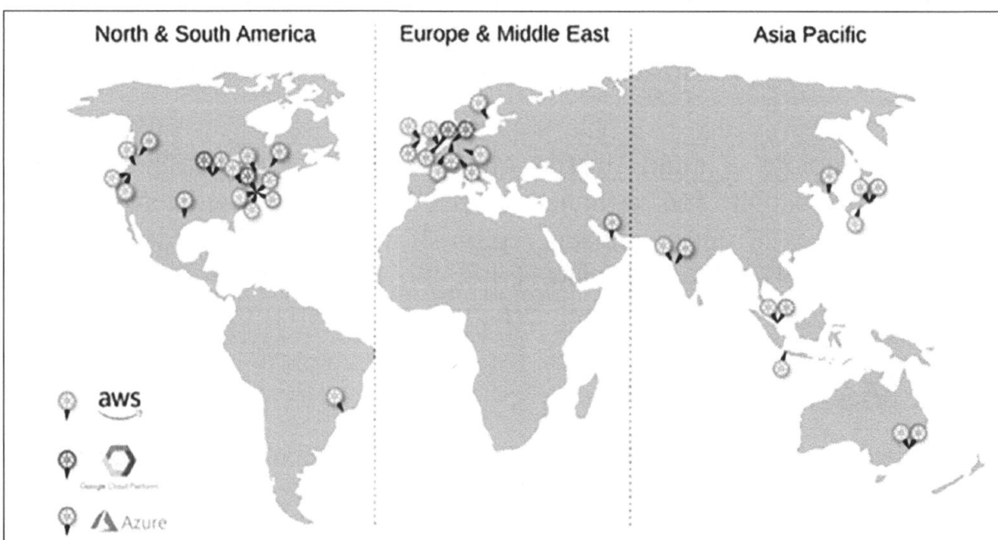

Figure 7.1: *Snowflake Regions*

(Source : https://docs.snowflake.com/en/user-guide/intro-regions as of Jan 2024, Snowflake adds more regions periodically so refer to this link for the latest)

Factors to Consider:

- Consider the location of your data sources and core users. Choose an area near these locations to reduce data transfer latency and improve query performance and user experience. If your data is mostly generated in Europe and your users are there, a European area may be advantageous.
- Companies in highly regulated industries including finance, healthcare, and government must comply with data residency rules. Make sure the region meets your company's and customers' data residency needs.
- Consider your company's downtime and data loss tolerance. Snowflake adds redundancy and data availability with cross-region replication. Consider your business continuity needs when choosing a region with enhanced availability or disaster recovery features.
- If you transmit large amounts of data between regions or cloud providers, data transfer expenses might build up. Consider data egress, ingress, and inter-region transfer fees for your region.
- Cloud compute and storage pricing vary by area. Compare Snowflake workload costs across regions to stay within budget.
- Various regions may have various Snowflake features and services. New features and upgrades may arrive early in some regions. To verify Snowflake features and services fit your needs, check their availability in your target location.
- Assess your company's data privacy and security laws. Some regions have tougher data protection rules, which may affect your data processing and security.
- Check Snowflake support and monitoring in your location. Local support teams can help solve problems and optimize performance.
- Consider future expansion and scalability for your company. As your organization grows, your region should handle more workloads and data.
- Assess data residency and compliance issues in your chosen region. If needed, consult legal and compliance professionals.
- Your data and business needs may warrant a multi-region strategy. Data is replicated between regions for redundancy and disaster recovery.
- Use Snowflake's built-in cross-region data replication and failover for high availability and disaster recovery.
- Monitor data transfer and cloud resource expenses in your location. Optimize data warehousing regularly to cut costs.

- Stay updated about Snowflake's regional feature availability and how it can benefit your company. Consider Snowflake's regional feature set while choosing.
- Choose an area for your company's growth. Select an area that can manage rising workloads and data volumes.
- Develop solid relationships with Snowflake's support teams and use their expertise for region-related choices.

The selection of the optimal Snowflake region for a Snowflake account is a strategic choice that necessitates meticulous evaluation of various aspects such as data proximity, compliance, redundancy, and cost. By evaluating your organization's distinct requirements and preferences, remaining knowledgeable about location-specific characteristics and advancements, and adopting recommended strategies for selecting a region, you can arrive at a well-informed choice that is in line with your objectives for data warehousing. This decision will guarantee optimal performance, adherence to regulations, and availability of data.

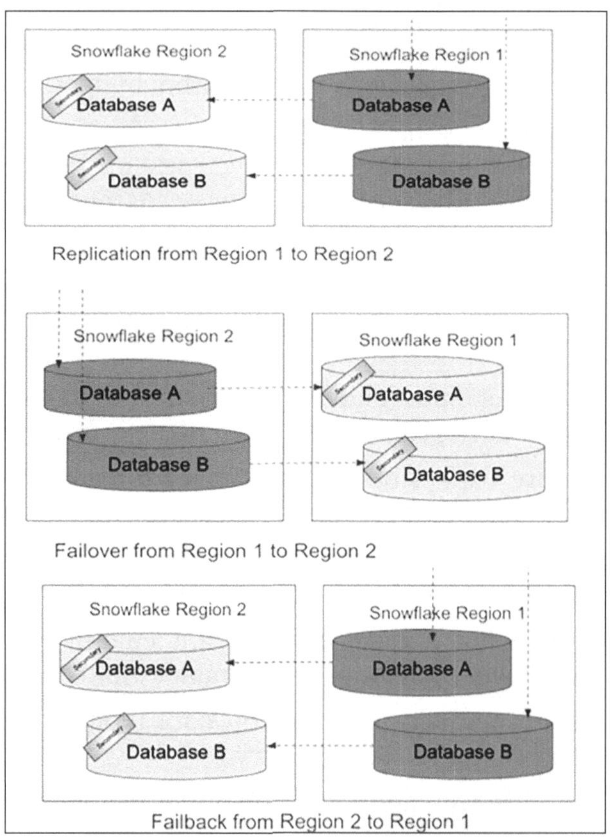

Figure 7.2: *Disaster Recovery in Snowflake*

In the preceding figure, the initial step entails establishing replication and failover to a distinct region, such as Region 2. In the event of an actual disaster, the database can be failed over to Region 2, making it the primary location for data loading until Region 1 is restored. Once Region 1 is operational again, a reverse replication process is executed to synchronize the databases. Subsequently, a failback to Region 1 is performed to resume normal operations.

Snowflake Multi-Region Disaster Recovery

Data management requires disaster recovery (DR) planning to ensure data availability and business continuity in the face of unforeseen catastrophes. Snowflake, a cloud-based data warehousing technology, offers multi-region data replication and failover for disaster recovery. Disaster recovery in Snowflake and multi-region recovery configuration are covered in this section.

Data is an asset of utmost importance for numerous organizations, and any interruption to the availability of data can result in significant ramifications. Snowflake acknowledges this concern and provides extensive disaster recovery features to limit potential hazards. There are several significant rationales for the criticality of disaster recovery in the context of Snowflake.

Disruptions to regular company operations can occur as a result of both natural and technological disasters. A robust disaster recovery strategy is critical for organizations to maintain uninterrupted access to and utilization of data, especially in challenging circumstances.

Data plays a crucial role in the functioning of contemporary organizations. The occurrence of data loss or unavailability can lead to adverse financial consequences, reputational harm, and legal ramifications. Disaster recovery measures are implemented to ensure the continuous availability of data, hence mitigating the risks associated with data loss and operational interruptions.

Numerous businesses and organizations are bound by stringent requirements pertaining to data governance and compliance. The implementation of a robust disaster recovery plan plays a crucial role in ensuring adherence to regulatory requirements through the preservation of data integrity and accessibility.

Customers have an inherent expectation that their data will be managed in a responsible and secure manner. The exhibition of a resilient catastrophe recovery strategy has the potential to foster trust and instill confidence throughout the client base.

Configuring a Multi-Region Recovery Strategy in Snowflake

Snowflake provides a data replication and failover capability known as **"Replication group and Failover groups"**, which enables the distribution of data across multiple regions. This functionality allows enterprises to duplicate data across many regions and transition to a backup area in the case of a catastrophic incident or the unavailability of a data center. This section presents a comprehensive guide on configuring a multi-region recovery strategy within the Snowflake data warehousing platform.

Please select a principal geographic area in which your primary Snowflake deployment will be located. Next, choose a secondary geographical area in which you would like to duplicate your data for disaster recovery. To mitigate the potential impact of simultaneous outages on both regions, it is advisable for the secondary region to be geographically away from the primary region.

To establish cross-region data replication in Snowflake, it is necessary to activate Cross cloud auto fulfillment. The aforementioned functionality enables users to effectively preserve a synchronized replica of their data in the secondary region.

The configuration of data replication rules involves the establishment of criteria to decide the selection of data objects, such as databases and tables, that will undergo replication from the primary region to the secondary region. The replication function of Snowflake guarantees the synchronization of modifications made in the primary region with the secondary region, achieving a state of near real-time mirroring.

The failover policies and procedures refer to the established guidelines and protocols that dictate the process of transitioning to the secondary region in the case of a failure in the primary region. This entails the establishment of DNS entries for the purpose of directing traffic to the secondary area, as well as the verification of the configuration of authentication and access constraints.

It is vital to conduct periodic assessments of your disaster recovery strategy, encompassing failover protocols, in order to ascertain the seamless transition of your firm to the secondary area in times of necessity. The procedure of testing plays a crucial role in the identification of potential faults and facilitates the subsequent improvement of the recovery process.

Incorporate resilient monitoring and alerting mechanisms to promptly identify and address potential problems on time. Snowflake offers monitoring functionalities that enable users to remain updated on the status and efficiency of their data replication and failover procedures.

Create comprehensive documentation of your disaster recovery plan, which should include detailed step-by-step procedures and contact information for essential individuals. It is imperative to provide comprehensive training to both the IT and operational teams to ensure the efficient implementation of the plan.

To ensure adherence, it is imperative to meticulously record and communicate the measures undertaken for disaster recovery. The provision of this paperwork holds significant importance in illustrating adherence to industry-specific legislation and organizational procedures.

It is imperative that disaster recovery strategies are not characterized by a stagnant nature. It is imperative to consistently evaluate and revise your plan to meet any modifications in your organization's infrastructure, data, or regulatory framework.

The advantages of using a multi-region recovery strategy are manifold. A well-designed multi-region recovery approach in Snowflake has numerous advantages

- High availability refers to the uninterrupted acccssibility of data, even in the event of a region experiencing a service disruption or outage.
- Data Protection: The replication and protection of data safeguards against potential data center failures or catastrophic events.
- Compliance: Ensures adherence to regulations pertaining to data residency and continuity.
- Business continuity aims to reduce downtime and guarantee uninterrupted business operations.
- Customer trust is established through a demonstration of dedication to data security and availability, thereby bolstering the confidence customers have in the organization.

The implementation of disaster recovery measures inside the Snowflake platform is an essential element of a holistic approach to data management. Organizations can achieve data availability, business continuity, and compliance while limiting risks related to data center failures or disasters by using a multi-region recovery strategy. Regular testing and maintenance of the disaster recovery plan are necessary in order to ascertain its efficacy during critical situations.

Conclusion

In summary, this chapter has provided insights into the essential factors that need to be taken into account when deploying Snowflake, with a specific emphasis on data management, region selection, and disaster recovery. The aforementioned factors serve as the fundamental pillars for establishing a robust and adaptable data architecture within the Snowflake platform.

Primarily, the importance of efficient data management cannot be overstated in the current era characterized by the reliance on data. It is imperative for organizations to engage in thorough planning when it comes to the processes of data intake, integration, modeling, and organization inside the Snowflake platform. This process guarantees the optimal storage and optimization of data, facilitating data-driven decision-making through analytics and reporting.

The selection of the Snowflake region is a matter that warrants careful consideration. The concept entails achieving a careful equilibrium among factors such as proximity to data sources and users, adherence to data residency regulations, financial considerations, and ensuring a high level of accessibility. The chosen geographical area should be in accordance with the organization's geographical and compliance requirements, while also taking into account cost-efficiency.

The chapter emphasizes that disaster recovery is an essential requirement rather than a discretionary option. Snowflake's multi-region recovery plan provides a resilient solution to guarantee the availability of data and the continuity of company operations in the event of unforeseen disruptions. One of the key benefits of this system is its ability to protect data from potential data center failures. Additionally, it contributes to the improvement of compliance measures and fosters a sense of confidence among customers.

In the current era characterized by a heavy reliance on data, where data has both value and susceptibility, the careful examination of these deployment factors assumes great significance. An intelligently designed data management strategy, in conjunction with careful region selection and a strong disaster recovery plan, establishes the basis for a durable and adaptable data infrastructure.

The ultimate achievement of a Snowflake deployment depends on the organization's capacity to achieve a harmonious equilibrium among data management effectiveness, data accessibility, and risk reduction. As enterprises persist in leveraging data for expansion and novelty, these factors will continue to be of utmost importance in their strategic planning within the Snowflake ecosystem.

The next chapter explores the fundamental principles underlying the effective management of data inside the Snowflake platform, which is characterized by a resilient and pioneering data storage architecture. Gaining a comprehensive understanding of the complexities associated with Snowflake's data storage is essential in order to fully leverage its capabilities.

It presents a thorough examination of Snowflake's distinctive data storage architecture, delving into its scalability, flexibility, and performance benefits. The chapter provides an analysis of the fundamental elements that form the foundation of Snowflake's storage system, including the division of storage and compute, the implementation of micro-partitions, and the utilization of clustering keys. By understanding these components, users can enhance their data storage strategies and effectively utilize the platform's capabilities.

Chapter 8

Data Storage in Snowflake

Introduction

Snowflake is a resilient and expandable storage framework that guarantees the effective storage, retrieval, and administration of data. Snowflake's data storage features encompass Time Travel, Clones, and data recovery procedures, enhancing data accessibility, flexibility, and robustness.

Snowflake's data storage paradigm is based on a unique architecture that segregates processing and storage. This segregation enables enterprises to expand their computational capabilities without affecting their storage capacity, leading to cost-effective and flexible data storage.

Time Travel is an essential aspect of Snowflake that allows users to retrieve previous versions of data. It facilitates the examination and troubleshooting of data modifications across time by allowing the capability to retrieve data as it existed at certain time intervals. Time Travel streamlines the procedures of data audits, compliance, and data recovery.

Clones in Snowflake allow users to generate autonomous duplicates of data for testing, development, and data exploration, among other objectives. They provide a cost-efficient approach to extracting knowledge from existing data without duplicating storage, as they utilize the same underlying data blocks as the original data.

Snowflake's data recovery techniques ensure the availability and durability of data. It intelligently duplicates data across many availability zones within a specific location, ensuring strong resistance to failures and long-lasting data preservation. Snowflake offers comprehensive data recovery solutions, such as point-in-time recovery and recovery from backups, to address data loss or inadvertent deletion.

By leveraging Snowflake's data storage features, including Time Travel, Clones, and data recovery mechanisms, enterprises can efficiently handle their data, examine past patterns, generate autonomous data copies, and guarantee the durability and accessibility of their data. Snowflake's extensive data storage capabilities empower enterprises to make informed decisions and extract valuable insights from their data assets.

Structure

In this chapter, the following topics will be covered:

- Snowflake Data Storage
- Snowflake Time Travel
- Snowflake Clones
- Data Recovery in Snowflake

Snowflake Data Storage

Snowflake, a data warehousing platform that operates in the cloud, provides a strong and adaptable architecture for storing data. This design is crucial for enabling Snowflake to deliver insights and manage data with exceptional performance. This section will provide an in-depth analysis of Snowflake's data storage capabilities, specifically examining its fundamental storage concepts, data management, and data preservation.

Snowflake utilizes a distinctive design that separates computational resources from storage, a principle referred to as separation of compute and storage. Traditional databases suffer from a tight coupling between compute and storage, which hampers scalability and flexibility. Snowflake stores data in an object store, such as Amazon S3, while virtual warehouses, which are computing clusters, grow independently to handle query processing. This division enables a storage capacity that is almost limitless and an ability to scale computing resources flexibly.

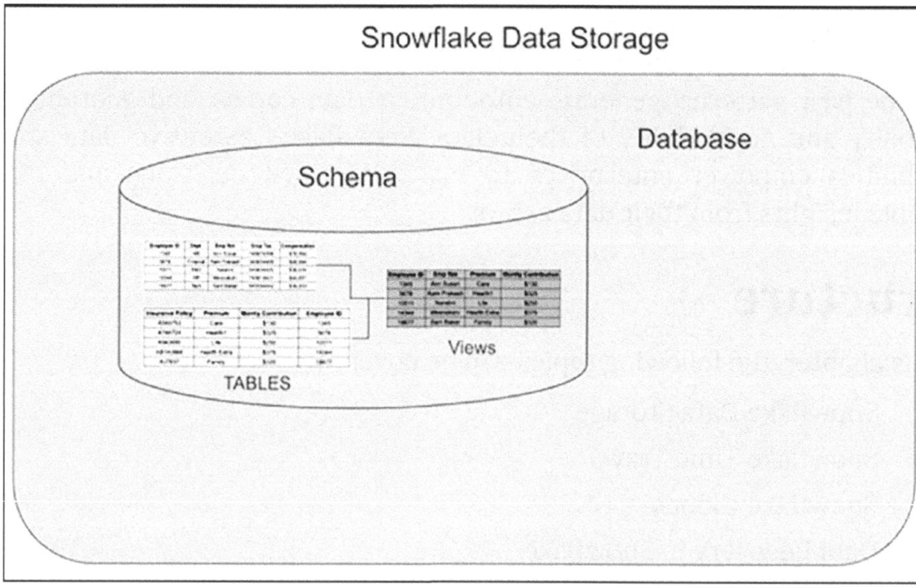

Figure 8.1: *Snowflake Storage Hierarchy*

Metadata is essential for the administration of data, and Snowflake stores metadata in a separate location from user data. By separating these components, the efficiency of query execution is maximized and the integrity of data processing is preserved. Metadata encompasses details regarding databases, tables, schemas, and user privileges.

Snowflake organizes data into databases and schemas. Databases serve as high-level repositories for data and can accommodate one or more schemas. Schemas encompass tables, views, and other objects within a database. The hierarchical structure facilitates the structuring of data and the implementation of access control measures.

Tables are the main objects used to store data in Snowflake, and they can be categorized into several types, such as standard tables, temporary tables, and external tables. Snowflake utilizes a columnar storage format instead of a row-based format, resulting in improved compression and query execution speed. In addition, Snowflake autonomously handles columnar storage formats, obviating the necessity for manual optimization.

Snowflake is capable of accommodating several data storage formats, such as Parquet, ORC, Avro, and JSON. These formats offer versatility for the intake and retrieval of data, while Snowflake optimizes the storage format automatically by analyzing usage patterns.

Snowflake utilizes columnar compression methods that effectively minimize storage demands. Query performance is enhanced by reading only the necessary columns, reducing data transfer. The metadata storage of Snowflake is exceptionally efficient, guaranteeing that metadata operations do not cause an increase in storage expenses. Snowflake autonomously handles data storage across many tiers, encompassing hot, cold, and archival storage, hence optimizing expenses according to data access patterns. This guarantees that data accessed frequently is stored in high-performance storage, while less frequently accessed data is transferred to cost-effective storage.

Snowflake places a high importance on data security and access control, guaranteeing the safeguarding of stored data. It implements Role-Based Access Control (RBAC) to effectively manage and control user permissions. One can establish roles, allocate rights, and regulate access to databases, schemas, and tables. Having granular control allows for the maintenance of data security and compliance. Snowflake uses encryption to secure data both when it is stored and when it is being transmitted. This encompasses the use of end-to-end encryption, which guarantees that data remains secure at all stages of its existence.

Efficient data governance depends on strong metadata management. Snowflake's metadata management capabilities offer a thorough perspective on the lineage, utilization, and access of data. This is extremely helpful for the management of data, ensuring adherence to regulations, and conducting audits. Snowflake effortlessly interacts with data catalogs, allowing enterprises to uphold a consolidated collection of metadata. This streamlines the process of finding data and promotes the implementation of efficient data management procedures.

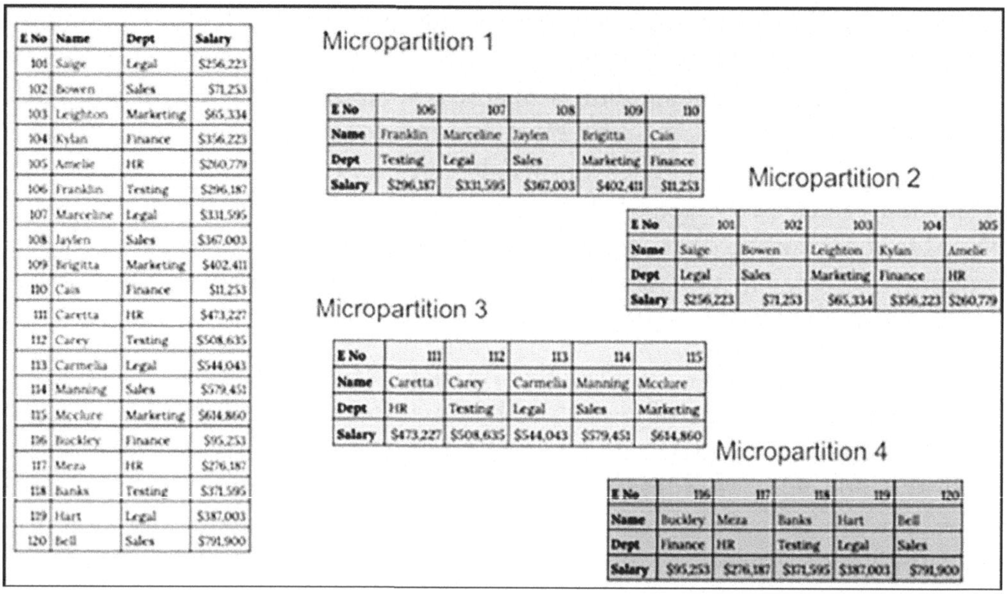

***Figure 8.2**: Snowflake Micropartition Hierarchy*

Snowflake Micropartition is a feature that improves data storage and query speed in the Snowflake data platform. It partitions data into smaller, more manageable chunks, allowing for increased effective data retrieval and processing. Snowflake Micropartition optimizes query performance and minimizes costs by structuring data at a more detailed level, which decreases the amount of data scanned during queries. This feature enhances scalability and enables users to study enormous datasets effortlessly. It enhances Snowflake's standing as a provider of efficient and economical data warehousing and analytics solutions, making it a vital resource for enterprises aiming for top-notch data management.

Snowflake's data storage capabilities, which are based on the principles of separating compute and storage, separating metadata, and organizing data efficiently, play a crucial role in its capacity to provide high-performance data warehousing and analytics. Snowflake allows enterprises to achieve a balance between performance and cost-effectiveness by automating data storage formats, optimizing compression, and providing storage tiering.

Ensuring data security and access control is of utmost importance, achieved through the use of RBAC and encryption to safeguard data. Effective data governance and compliance are enhanced by the use of strong metadata management and seamless connection with data catalogs.

The data storage capabilities of Snowflake are essential to its status as a top-tier data warehousing platform. They enable enterprises to efficiently, safely, and compliantly manage, store, and analyze data. Comprehending and utilizing these abilities is crucial for unlocking the complete potential of Snowflake to make data-informed decisions and achieve organizational success.

Snowflake Time Travel

The Time Travel feature of Snowflake is a robust capability that distinguishes it from other data warehousing solutions. It provides customers with the capability to get data at various time intervals, allowing them to gain temporal insights into their data. This section provides an in-depth examination of Snowflake Time Travel, including its functionality, practical applications, and recommended strategies for optimizing its benefits.

Time Travel in Snowflake enables the retrieval of past iterations of data stored in a table. It enables you to access and analyze data from a certain time in the past or future, allowing for rewinding and querying. This function is revolutionary for firms aiming to assess data modifications, resolve problems, and adhere to audit and regulatory obligations.

Snowflake Time Travel functions by utilizing two separate characteristics: Time Travel and Data Retention.

- Time Travel enables the user to retrieve data in its historical or future state. It offers two modes:
    - **Point-in-Time (PIT) Query**: This mode allows you to retrieve data as it was at a particular timestamp in the past. By specifying the desired timestamp, Snowflake will deliver a precise snapshot of the data at that particular moment.
    - **Relative Time Travel**: This feature allows you to journey to either the past or the future in relation to the present moment. As an illustration, you have the capability to retrieve data from 7 days ago or 2 hours in the future. This is very advantageous for conducting trend analysis and making predictions.
- Data Retention is intricately linked to the concept of Time Travel. Snowflake maintains historical data by keeping several versions of modified or removed rows. The ability to retain data can be adjusted at the level of individual tables. When a Time Travel query is executed, Snowflake gets the pertinent data according to the retention policy that has been set.

The adaptability of Snowflake Time travel presents numerous potential applications:

- **Data auditing and ensuring compliance with regulations**: Time travel enables data auditing by providing companies with the ability to monitor and record alterations made to data throughout different points in time. This is essential for guaranteeing adherence to regulatory obligations such as GDPR, HIPAA, or industry-specific benchmarks.
- **Problem-solving and identifying errors**: Time travel allows data experts to analyze data in its state at the time when issues occurred, facilitating the investigation of problems. This can accelerate the process of identifying and resolving problems, as well as determining the underlying reason.
- **Data recovery**: It refers to the process of retrieving lost or inaccessible data from storage devices. Time Travel can be a valuable tool in situations involving data corruption or unintentional erasure, perhaps saving one's digital existence. Users can retrieve lost data by searching a previous iteration of the impacted table.
- **Examining past data patterns and predicting future trends:** This is essential for making decisions based on data. Time Travel facilitates this process by offering convenient access to historical data.
- **A/B testing**: It refers to a method of comparing two versions of a webpage or app to see which one performs better in terms of user engagement or conversion rates. Time Travel enables businesses to compare the outcomes of A/B tests conducted to assess changes in user behavior or product features, both before and after the test.

To optimize the utilization of Snowflake Time Travel, it is advisable to adhere to the following recommended procedures:

- Set up the parameters for storing and maintaining data over a specific period of time.
- Customize data retention policies according to the specific requirements of your organization. Extended retention periods yield a greater amount of historical data for study, albeit at the potential expense of increased storage expenses. Consistently evaluate and modify retention strategies to achieve optimal equilibrium.
- Although Time Travel possesses significant capabilities, it is crucial to use prudent discretion when employing it. Overutilization might result in longer query durations and higher resource use. To optimize resource utilization, it is essential to provide the precise timestamp or time frame required.

- Track and evaluate the efficiency of database queries. Time travel inquiries may exhibit distinct performance characteristics compared to standard inquiries. Monitor the performance and resource utilization of queries in order to detect and resolve any bottlenecks that may affect performance.
- To optimize the retrieval of historical data that is viewed frequently, it is advisable to generate materialized views. Precomputed views can enhance the efficiency of Time Travel queries by minimizing the requirement to scan extensive datasets.
- Establish data cleansing and archiving strategies to efficiently manage the lifecycle of data. Eliminate obsolete or duplicate data to minimize storage expenses and uphold data currency.
- Instruct your data users on the functionalities and correct utilization of Snowflake Time Travel. Develop comprehensive documentation and training materials to optimize user utilization of this feature while maintaining system performance integrity.

Constraints of Snowflake Time Travel

Although Snowflake Time Travel possesses significant capabilities, it is crucial to acknowledge its constraints:

- **Storage costs**: Storing previous iterations of historical data can result in higher expenses for storage. Organizations must diligently oversee data retention rules to strike a balance between the availability of historical data and cost-effectiveness.
- **Query efficiency:** Time Travel queries may experience significantly longer query durations in comparison to ordinary searches, particularly when retrieving substantial amounts of previous data. Monitoring the performance of queries is essential for optimizing the utilization of resources.
- **Resource consumption**: Time travel queries that are complex and require several joins and aggregations might consume a significant amount of resources. Make sure that your data warehouse is appropriately sized to accommodate these queries.

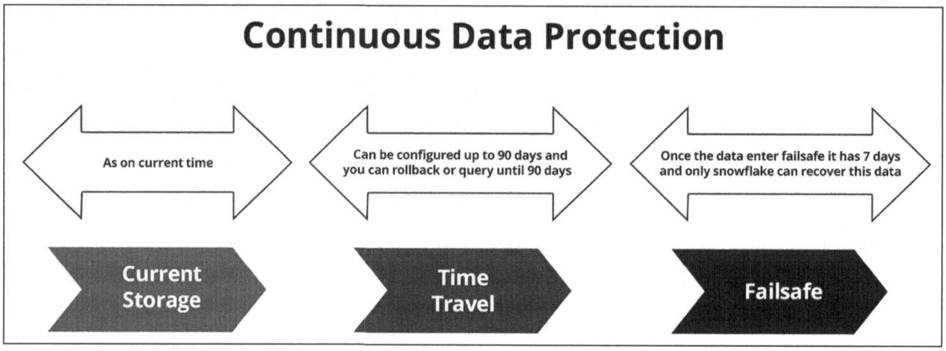

Figure 8.3: *Time Travel in Snowflake Hierarchy*

The Snowflake Time Travel feature is a revolutionary capability that enables enterprises to fully leverage the value of their past data. Time Travel offers the ability to examine historical and future data for purposes such as auditing, troubleshooting, recovery, trend research, or A/B testing.

Organizations can harness the capabilities of Snowflake Time Travel, optimize storage costs, and enhance query performance by implementing data retention policies, employing Time Travel strategically, and following recommended guidelines.

Snowflake Clones

Snowflake provides a feature called **Clones** that is essential for optimizing various data-related tasks, particularly in the areas of testing and development. This section provides a detailed examination of Snowflake Clones, elucidating their functionality, examining their practical applications, and offering recommendations for optimizing their utilization.

Snowflake Clones are essentially immutable, precise duplicates of a database, schema, or table within a Snowflake account. These clones possess a low weight, indicating that they utilize the identical underlying data storage as the original object. Nevertheless, they offer a distinct and secluded setting for conducting tests, developing applications, analyzing data, or engaging in any other task without affecting the original data.

Cloning in Snowflake entails generating a snapshot of the metadata of the source object and a reference to the data that is shared. This results in a highly efficient procedure in terms of both storage and resource use. Upon creation, a clone does not initially require any additional storage. Conversely, it utilizes the identical storage as the source object. The clone undergoes changes, such as alterations to the data, and only the updated data is duplicated and stored independently, following the **copy-on-write** process. This reduces the amount of storage space required.

Data isolation refers to the practice of keeping data separate and protected from unauthorized access or modification. Clones offer a completely separate and self-contained habitat. Modifications performed on a clone, such as the insertion, modification, or removal of data, are kept separate from the original object and other clones. This guarantees that testing or development operations do not compromise the integrity of the source data.

Clones acquire the schema and metadata of the original object, thereby retaining the structure and organization of the data by replicating tables, views, and other database objects.

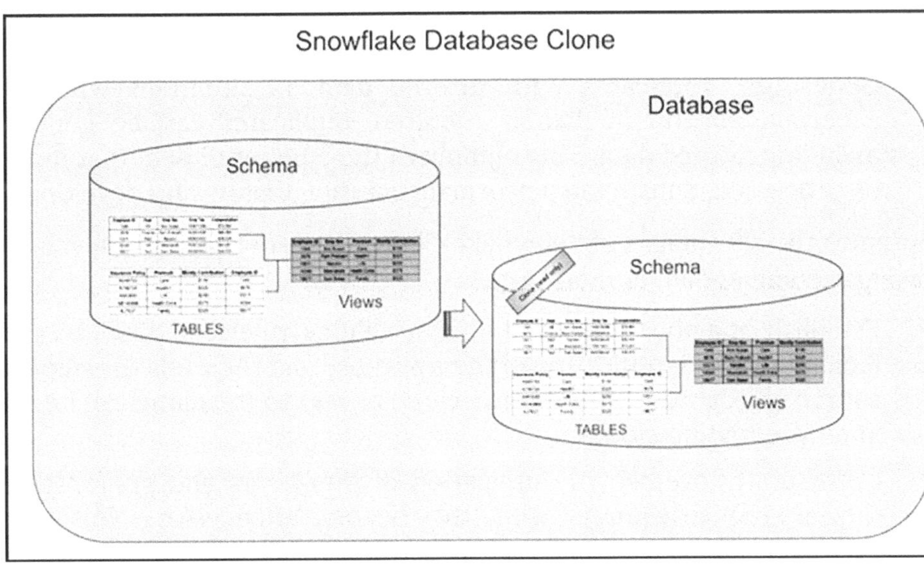

***Figure 8.4**: Database Clones in Snowflake Hierarchy*

Applications of Snowflake Clones

Snowflake Clones have a diverse range of applications, primarily aimed at improving testing and development procedures. Here are several typical situations in which clones can be quite useful:

- **Testing of data-driven apps, analytics models, and ETL operations:** Clones facilitate comprehensive testing of data-driven apps, analytics models, and

ETL operations without affecting production data. QA teams can verify modifications, detect problems, and guarantee the precision of data.

- **Creating and testing preliminary version:** Clones help in the process of creating and testing a preliminary version of a product or system. Data developers have the ability to produce duplicates in order to construct and evaluate new functionalities, database configurations, or SQL inquiries within a separate and controlled setting. This serves to mitigate any inadvertent repercussions on the primary dataset.
- **Analysis and presentation of data**: Analysts and data scientists can utilize clones to investigate data, construct intricate queries, and produce reports. Clones offer a secure environment for conducting data exploration without impacting real-time data.
- **Ensuring adherence to rules and regulations and conducting audits**: Clones can be employed for the goal of ensuring adherence to rules and regulations, as well as for conducting audits. Organizations can retain historical records of data to adhere to regulatory requirements, conduct internal audits, or perform forensic analysis.
- **Generating duplicates with filtered data:** In situations where only a certain portion of data is required, duplicates can be generated, including filtered data. This minimizes the amount of data that needs to be processed, enhancing performance during testing and development.

To optimize the advantages of Snowflake Clones, it is advisable to adhere to the following recommended methodologies:

- Establish unambiguous and uniform naming rules for duplicates. This facilitates the identification of their purpose and their relationship to the source object. Adding the words **clone** or **test** to the name can be useful in differentiating clones.
- Consistently oversee the utilization of duplicates and guarantee that they are regularly purged when they become unnecessary. This helps to save superfluous expenses for storage and reduces disorder.
- Ensure the existence of documentation that clearly outlines the purpose, ownership, and lifecycle of every clone. This documentation facilitates comprehension of the function and importance of each clone.
- Enforce suitable access restrictions for duplicates. Implement strict access controls to restrict the creation or modification of clones to authorized users, thereby mitigating the risk of misuse.
- It is advisable to establish procedures for regularly updating clones with the most recent data from the original object. This guarantees that clones maintain consistency with the most up-to-date data.

Although Snowflake Clones provide significant advantages, it is crucial to acknowledge their limitations. Clones are restricted to viewing or accessing information without the ability to make changes or modifications. They possess an inherent characteristic of being immutable, which means modifications made to a clone do not transfer back to the original item. This restriction is intentionally implemented to guarantee the separation and reliability of data. While clones are storage-efficient, thanks to the copy-on-write method, they still require storage space. It is crucial to effectively manage and monitor the expenses associated with storage. Clones acquire the structure of the original item when they are created. However, modifications to the schema of the original object do not automatically propagate to pre-existing clones. Recreating clones may be necessary to synchronize them with revised schemas.

Snowflake Clones revolutionize the field of data warehousing by providing a highly efficient and isolated environment for a range of data-related tasks, with a special focus on testing and development. By utilizing the copy-on-write process, clones achieve a harmonious combination of data segregation and storage efficiency.

Organizations can optimize the utilization of clones by adhering to established guidelines, thereby enhancing data accuracy, expediting development processes, and safeguarding the integrity of production data during testing activities. Snowflake enables data professionals to enhance their data-driven projects by providing them with clones, which in turn allows for more agility and efficiency.

Data Recovery in Snowflake

Data recovery is an essential component of every data management system, guaranteeing that companies can retrieve and reinstate data in case of inadvertent deletions, data corruptions, or other unexpected problems. Snowflake provides resilient data recovery capabilities that not only protect data but also give a Fail-Safe way for data retrieval. This section will provide a thorough examination of Snowflake Data Recovery, including its functionality, importance, and the procedure for recovering data from Fail-Safe. Additionally, it will discuss the expenses and factors to consider in relation to this process.

Snowflake Data Recovery is specifically developed to guarantee the accessibility and reliability of your data in a range of different situations, as follows:

- Data may be inadvertently erased by users or software. The data recovery feature of Snowflake enables the retrieval of lost data, as long as it remains within the designated retention period.

- Data corruption can arise infrequently as a result of problems in data processing, device malfunctions, or other contributing causes. Snowflake's data recovery service enables the restoration of data to a prior condition, free from any corruption.
- Snowflake's data recovery feature allows users to retrieve historical data, giving them the ability to access data exactly as it existed at certain time points. This feature is extremely important for the purposes of auditing, compliance, or historical analysis.

Fail-Safe serves as a supplementary level of safeguarding data. The Fail-Safe layer in Snowflake maintains a complete and unchangeable record of every modification made to the data. This layer functions as a protective measure against the loss of data. Deleted data that exceeds the Time Travel retention period can still be recovered from the Fail-Safe layer. Retrieving data from the Fail-Safe layer is feasible, but it necessitates taking specific factors into account:

- Extracting information from the Fail-Safe layer can require a significant amount of resources and incur high expenses. The reason for this is that Fail-Safe data is stored in a highly condensed and unchangeable format, which necessitates extra computational resources to restore.
- Retrieving data from the Fail-Safe layer can be time-consuming, particularly for extensive datasets. Snowflake needs to restore the data from its compressed form, which may lead to slower retrieval times in comparison to standard queries.
- Obtaining data from the Fail-Safe layer necessitates aid from Snowflake support. To commence the retrieval process, users must file a support ticket and collaborate with Snowflake's support team.
- Snowflake imposes supplementary charges for the retrieval of data through the Fail-Safe mechanism. The expenses can fluctuate depending on the amount of data being recovered and the intricacy of the retrieval procedure.

To optimize Snowflake Data Recovery and guarantee data availability and integrity, it is advisable to adhere to the following recommended procedures:

- Acquire a comprehensive understanding of Snowflake's data retention policies, which encompass the Time Travel and Fail-Safe retention durations. Ensure that these policies are in accordance with the data recovery and compliance requirements of your firm.
- It is advisable to incorporate regular data backups to reduce reliance on data recovery from the Fail-Safe layer. Backups offer an extra level of safeguarding for data.

- Regularly assess the data recovery procedure to verify its ability to efficiently retrieve data as required. Testing facilitates the detection and resolution of any potential faults in the recovery cycle.
- Consider the expenses associated with data recovery, particularly from the Fail-Safe layer. Devise and allocate funds appropriately to prevent unforeseen expenditures.
- Adopt resilient data governance measures to mitigate the risk of inadvertent data deletions and data corruptions.
- Provide users with comprehensive information on optimal data handling techniques to avoid the necessity for data recovery.

Snowflake Data Recovery plays a vital role in the platform's data management capabilities. It guarantees the availability, integrity, and historical access of data, giving organizations the assurance that their data is safeguarded even in unforeseen circumstances.

Although the retrieval of data from the Fail-Safe layer is a valuable technique for ensuring safety in case of failure, it should be employed with caution due to its high resource requirements and associated costs. Organizations must find a harmonious equilibrium between their data recovery requirements and their efforts to control costs to maximize their data recovery approach.

Snowflake's Data Recovery capabilities enable enterprises to ensure data resilience and accessibility, protecting their most precious asset—data—in the dynamic field of data management and compliance.

Data Retention Policies

Snowflake, a cloud-based data warehousing platform, implements a thorough data retention policy that determines the duration for which historical data is retained in the system. Data retention policies typically focus on ensuring compliance, but they also greatly influence query performance and data management. This section will explore Snowflake's data retention policy, its impact on query performance, and ideas for optimizing data retention in businesses.

Time Travel is a functionality that enables users to retrieve data from a certain moment in the past or future. Snowflake stores previous versions of data for a specific amount of time, as determined by the Time Travel retention period setting. The duration of this period can be customized and adjusted at both the account and table levels.

The account-level retention policy establishes a predetermined amount of time during which all tables within the account are retained. Tables automatically adopt this retention duration unless it is specifically modified at the table level.

Administrators can set distinct Time Travel retention periods for specific tables, allowing for more precise management. This is especially advantageous when specific tables necessitate varying retention periods that are either shorter or longer, depending on the requirements of the organization.

The Fail-Safe layer of Snowflake preserves all past iterations of data, guaranteeing the integrity and recoverability of the data. This layer serves as a protective measure against data loss, even in cases when data exceeds the Time Travel retention period. The duration of Fail-Safe retention is generally much greater than that of Time Travel retention. However, it cannot be customized by the user and is controlled by Snowflake.

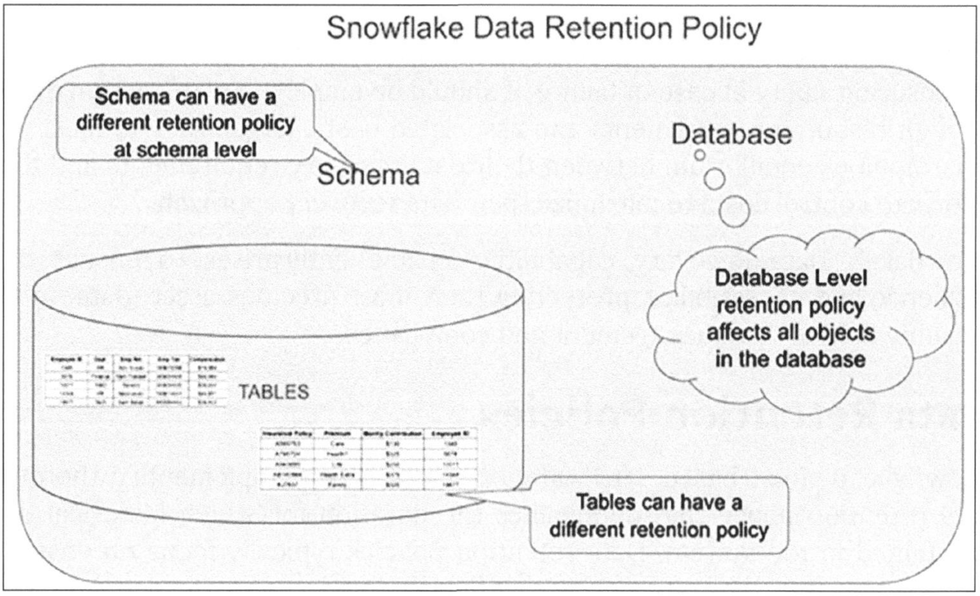

Figure 8.5: *Data Retention Policy Hierarchy*

The data retention policy of Snowflake has many ramifications on the performance of queries:

- Organizations can enhance query performance by designating a reduced Time Travel retention time for particular tables. Reducing the duration of data retention periods decreases the amount of past data that Snowflake needs to examine while processing queries, resulting in quicker response times.

- Adjusting the duration for which Time Travel data is retained enhances storage efficiency. Extended retention durations result in higher storage demands, whereas shorter periods enhance storage efficiency. Organizations can optimize storage expenses while ensuring data accessibility according to their own requirements.
- Reducing the retention durations for time travel results in decreased resource consumption when executing queries. This is particularly beneficial in scenarios where computationally demanding queries must be handled expeditiously.
- Reducing the duration of Time Travel retention periods guarantees that the data being queried is more up-to-date. Access to the most up-to-date data is crucial for real-time analytics, reporting, and decision-making processes.

To maximize the benefits of Snowflake's data preservation policy and improve query performance, it is advisable to implement the following optimization strategies:

- Establish the suitable duration for retaining Time Travel data for each table, taking into consideration its usage and significance. To optimize storage and enhance query performance, choose shorter retention periods for tables containing less crucial data.
- Regularly assess and modify Time Travel storage configurations to match evolving business needs. As the amount of data increases and the ways in which it is used change, it may be necessary to modify your retention policy.
- Utilize the Fail-Safe layer to meet long-term data retention and regulatory requirements. This enables you to preserve access to old data without compromising storage or query performance.
- Ensure that your data retention policies are well documented and effectively communicated within your organization. This guarantees that all parties involved are informed about the policies and their influence on query performance and data accessibility.
- Establish monitoring and alert systems to ensure adherence to data retention regulations. Alerts can inform administrators when tables are nearing or surpassing their Time Travel retention periods, motivating immediate action.

The data retention policy of Snowflake is a versatile tool that fulfills both compliance and query performance optimization objectives. By customizing the duration for which Time Travel retains data to align with the unique requirements of your company, you may achieve a harmonious equilibrium between the accessibility of data, efficiency of storage, and performance of queries.

Continuously improving data retention strategies necessitates regular evaluation and modification. As your organization's data environment changes, it is important to consider how data preservation affects query performance. This will help you maximize the benefits of Snowflake's robust data warehousing capabilities while also meeting compliance and data management needs.

Managing Snowflake Storage Cost

Snowflake provides a variety of functionalities to enhance storage efficiency and manage expenses. An effective strategy for controlling Snowflake storage expenses involves utilizing metadata tables, which are highly influential tools.

These tables offer essential information about your storage consumption, enabling you to make well-informed choices and take steps to optimize storage expenses.

Snowflake offers a collection of predefined metadata tables that record comprehensive data and storage consumption statistics:

- The term **`INFORMATION_SCHEMA`** refers to a database schema that provides information about the structure and contents of a database. The schema encompasses metadata tables that offer comprehensive information about many elements of your Snowflake environment, such as tables, columns, views, and storage utilization.
- **`SNOWFLAKE.ACCOUNT_USAGE`**: This schema provides a comprehensive overview of resource utilization at the account level, encompassing storage consumption and query history.
- The **`SNOWFLAKE.ACCOUNT_USAGE.QUERY_HISTORY`** view records past query data, enabling the analysis of query performance and resource usage.
- The **`SNOWFLAKE.ACCOUNT_USAGE.STORAGE_USAGE`** view offers comprehensive data on storage utilization at both the table and schema levels.

Following are several techniques for effectively controlling Snowflake storage expenses through the utilization of metadata tables:

- Utilize the **`SNOWFLAKE.ACCOUNT_USAGE.STORAGE_USAGE`** view to examine the amount of storage used by individual tables and schemas. This table offers a comprehensive overview of the storage usage for each individual table and schema. Identify tables exhibiting significant storage use and evaluate the necessity of all stored data.
- Utilize the **`SNOWFLAKE.ACCOUNT_USAGE`** schema to examine past usage trends. Analyze patterns in storage utilization and query logs. This data can assist in predicting future storage requirements and identifying possibilities for optimization.

- Determine tables that are now unused or have become outdated. Utilize metadata tables to ascertain the most recent instance of when a table was accessed or modified. If a table becomes obsolete, it is advisable to either archive or delete it to release storage capacity.
- When generating clones for testing or development purposes, it is important to consider their storage implications. Initially, clones and the original object have the same storage. However, as modifications are done, extra storage may be used. To minimize excessive storage expenses, it is important to consistently monitor and eliminate unwanted clones.
- Deploy monitoring and alert systems utilizing metadata tables to remain updated on storage utilization patterns. Configure alerts to promptly tell you when storage usage exceeds predetermined criteria, enabling timely intervention.
- If you have historical data that is infrequently accessed but has to be stored for compliance or other reasons, you might consider utilizing Snowflake's data archiving capabilities. Migrate older data to more economical storage tiers while maintaining its accessibility for future use.
- Assess and modify your storage rules in Snowflake to correspond with your organization's goals for data retention and cost reduction. Optimize storage expenses by customizing the retention periods and Fail-Safe procedures for Time Travel.

Utilizing metadata tables in Snowflake offers numerous advantages in effectively managing storage expenses:

- **Transparency**: Metadata tables provide clear visibility into your data and storage utilization, enabling you to make well-informed choices regarding storage optimization.
- **Data-driven insights**: By analyzing previous usage data, you may gain a comprehensive understanding of trends and patterns, which in turn allows for proactive management of storage.
- **Cost optimization**: By identifying dormant or suboptimally stored data, you can minimize superfluous storage expenses.
- **Performance optimization**: Implementing data compression and archiving techniques can enhance query performance and minimize resource usage.
- **Compliance and governance**: Metadata tables facilitate compliance and governance by monitoring data utilization and maintaining a record of data access history.

Efficiently controlling Snowflake storage expenses is crucial for enhancing the performance of your data warehousing infrastructure. By utilizing Snowflake's metadata tables, you can obtain vital information about storage usage, past usage patterns, and opportunities for optimizing resources. By implementing data-driven strategies, you can effectively decrease storage expenses while ensuring continued data accessibility and compliance. Periodically evaluate and modify your storage management strategies to maintain continuous cost control and efficiency in your Snowflake implementation.

When working in Snowflake, the selection of table types – temporary, transient, or permanent – relies on criteria such as data retention requirements, query speed, and resource consumption. Understanding the distinctions among these table categories and taking into account Snowflake's time travel capability can assist in making well-informed decisions.

Temporary tables are suitable for storing data that is only required for a session or a particular job. They are automatically deleted at the end of a session, which helps to release resources and minimize storage expenses. They are beneficial for intermediate data processing or staging tasks where data persistence is unnecessary after the current session.

Transient tables are ideal for storing transient data that must persist across sessions but are not essential for long-term storage. Transient tables endure until expressly removed or for a set time-to-live (TTL) period, unlike temporary tables. They offer flexibility in handling transient data while reducing storage overhead.

Permanent tables are intended for storing enduring data that necessitates durability and consistency across time. These tables are resilient and remain intact across sessions. Permanent tables are ideal for storing transactional data, historical records, or reference data that must be kept for analysis, reporting, or preservation purposes.

Snowflake's time travel feature enhances table selection by adding another dimension. Time travel enables users to access past data at various time points, offering insights on data modifications and facilitating data auditing and compliance. When selecting table kinds, it is crucial to evaluate the Time Travel needs and select the suitable retention duration (for example, number of days) according to data governance policies and regulatory compliance requirements.

Ultimately, the choice of tables in Snowflake – temporary, transient, or permanent – depends on criteria such as data permanence, session duration, and time travel needs. Users may optimize data management and resource consumption in their Snowflake environment by understanding the distinctions between table types and the consequences of Snowflake's time travel functionality.

Conclusion

Ultimately, Snowflake's Data Storage, Time Travel, Clones, and Data Recovery functionalities combine to create a strong and all-encompassing framework for managing and safeguarding data. This chapter has examined the interplay of these components in order to guarantee the integrity of data, facilitate its accessibility, and optimize resource consumption within the Snowflake cloud data warehousing platform.

Snowflake employs a very efficient and scalable technique for storing data. By separating computing and storage, companies have the ability to expand their compute resources independently, and they are only charged for the storage they really use. This elasticity reduces operational expenses and enables smooth scalability as data requirements increase.

Snowflake's Data Recovery capabilities, such as Time Travel and Fail-Safe, are crucial measures to protect against data loss and corruption. Fail-Safe guarantees the preservation of past iterations of data, even beyond the expiration of the Time Travel retention period. Nevertheless, enterprises should be cognizant of the expenses and resource requirements involved in obtaining data from the Fail-Safe layer.

Collectively, these attributes enable enterprises to efficiently oversee their data, striking a balance between the requirement for accessing past data, optimizing storage, and controlling costs. Organizations can optimize their utilization of Snowflake's data management features by adhering to best practices for data preservation, clone management, and storage optimization.

Snowflake's approach to data storage, preservation, and accessibility establishes a solid basis for enterprises to fully leverage their data in the quickly changing field of data management and analytics. Snowflake's features encompass a range of capabilities, including real-time analytics, compliance assurance, and resource utilization optimization. These tools enable data-driven success while upholding the utmost standards of data integrity and security.

The upcoming chapter explores the Snowflake Data Marketplaces, which have emerged as platforms facilitating the sharing and commercialization of data, enabling companies to identify, access, and utilize a wide range of data sources for analytical and business objectives. The Data Marketplace offered by Snowflake is a powerful tool that allows businesses to easily find and use a wide range of external datasets. This helps them improve their own data resources and increase their ability to analyze data.

CHAPTER 9
Snowflake Marketplace

Introduction

Snowflake Marketplace are platforms that enable the sharing and monetization of data, enabling companies to identify, access, and utilize a wide range of data sources for analytical and business objectives. This powerful tool enables businesses to find and use a wide range of third-party datasets, which helps them improve their own data resources and increase their ability to analyze data.

To understand Snowflake's Marketplace, it is essential to analyze its architecture. The foundation of Snowflake's Marketplace is a robust and expandable infrastructure that allows data providers to publish and distribute their datasets, while ensuring data consumers can effortlessly discover and access them. The architecture establishes a reliable setting for the flow of data by guaranteeing confidentiality, adherence to regulations, and proper management of data.

By utilizing Snowflake's Marketplace, customers can leverage its data discovery and search functionalities to explore and identify pertinent datasets tailored to their individual objectives. The utilization of advanced search functionalities, metadata identifiers, and data profile information enables customers to accurately determine the most suitable datasets for their analytics projects.

The Snowflake Marketplace facilitates data vendors in publishing their datasets through listing and publication processes. Data providers have the ability to establish data standards, access controls, and price mechanisms for their datasets. In addition, they have the ability to manage and refresh their listings, guaranteeing that data consumers obtain precise and up-to-date information.

Through the utilization of Snowflake's Marketplace, enterprises may gain access to an extensive ecosystem of carefully selected and dependable datasets.

This enables them to expedite their data-driven efforts and obtain significant insights. The Marketplace architecture offers a seamless and secure platform for companies to discover, access, and utilize third-party data to enhance their own data assets. This is achieved through the integration of data discovery, search capabilities, and data listing processes.

Structure

In this chapter, the following topics will be covered:

- Understanding Snowflake's Marketplace
- Marketplace Architecture
- Data Discovery and Search
- Data Listing and Publication
- Prerequisite for Listing on Marketplace

Understanding Snowflake's Marketplace

The Snowflake Marketplace is an online platform that enables data suppliers to securely share their datasets with a diverse array of data consumers. The Snowflake Data Cloud effortlessly incorporates it, serving as a worldwide data-sharing platform that links companies and data providers to an extensive and varied assortment of data resources.

Notable Characteristics of Snowflake's Marketplace:

- **Data Collaboration:** Data suppliers can publish their datasets on the marketplace, thereby granting access to a worldwide audience of data consumers. This facilitates the effective exchange of data and cooperation.

***Figure 9.1**: Marketplace Hierarchy*

- **Data Discovery**: This is key as users can search and explore datasets from a diverse range of sources, sectors, and domains. The marketplace provides comprehensive metadata and descriptions to assist users in locating the appropriate data.
- **Secure Data Exchange**: Data is securely exchanged within the Snowflake Data Cloud, guaranteeing the protection of sensitive information. Data is protected by the use of access controls and encryption techniques. Data suppliers can generate revenue from their datasets by establishing price and licensing conditions. This allows data providers to gain income from their data assets.
- **Data Integration**: The marketplace offers the ability to track and report on how data providers' datasets are being utilized and by whom. Data integration is the smooth integration of datasets from the marketplace into Snowflake's data platform. This allows customers to merge external data with their internal datasets, facilitating complete analysis.
- **Revenue Generation**: Data providers have the opportunity to generate revenue from their data assets by offering them for sale on the marketplace. This creates additional sources of income and possibilities for data providers to profit from their data investments.
- **Increased Accessibility**: The marketplace grants entry to a worldwide pool of potential data consumers. Data suppliers can expand their consumer reach and enhance the influence of their data.

- **Usage Insights**: Data providers obtain vital insights regarding the utilization of their datasets through Usage Insights. This information can assist them in enhancing their data offerings and refining their pricing strategies. The marketplace provides a wide array of datasets from different businesses and topics. Data consumers can retrieve data from external sources to enhance their analyses.
- **Streamlining Data Search and Acquisition:** The Snowflake platform enhances efficiency by streamlining data search and acquisition, hence minimizing the time and effort needed to locate and integrate external data. Snowflake ensures the veracity and dependability of datasets on the marketplace, guaranteeing that consumers can have confidence in the data they retrieve.
- **Impact on the Data Ecosystem** The Marketplace developed by Snowflake has had a substantial influence on the data ecosystem. It enables organizations, regardless of their size or industry, to access high-quality datasets that were previously difficult to obtain, thus democratizing data access. Data providers, such as businesses and individuals, now have a fresh opportunity to generate revenue from their data assets. This promotes the sharing of data and fosters the development of valuable datasets. Data users can effortlessly obtain and incorporate external data, expediting their data-centric insights and decision-making procedures.
- **Facilitating Cooperation between Businesses:** The marketplace facilitates cooperation between businesses, allowing them to efficiently exchange and utilize data resources. Snowflake's strong security and access control methods guarantee that data is shared and accessed in a manner that complies with regulations and is regulated effectively, hence improving data governance procedures.

The Marketplace developed by Snowflake is a revolutionary platform that significantly transforms the landscape of data exchange, availability, and commercialization. This platform enables data suppliers to generate revenue from their resources and offers data consumers a wide range of varied datasets, promoting cooperation within the data ecosystem. With the ongoing evolution of the marketplace, it is expected to have a crucial impact on promoting data-driven innovation and providing valuable insights across many industries. This makes it an essential tool for companies aiming to harness the potential of data.

Snowflake Marketplace Architecture

The Snowflake Marketplace is an exceptional platform that enables the effortless sharing and utilization of data assets inside the Snowflake ecosystem. In order to facilitate this capability, it utilizes an advanced framework that guarantees the secure transmission of information while also preserving efficiency and expandability.

The infrastructure of the Snowflake Marketplace is designed and optimized for cloud computing environments. It is founded upon a cloud-native infrastructure. Snowflake is a cloud-native data warehousing platform that operates on well-known cloud providers such as AWS, Azure, and GCP. This architecture exploits the scalability, flexibility, and reliability of these cloud platforms.

Snowflake utilizes a deployment methodology that involves multiple clusters and regions. This implies that it can extend over various geographical areas and data centers to guarantee the availability of data, facilitate disaster recovery, and provide users worldwide with fast access. This architecture plays a vital role in the Marketplace by ensuring the secure sharing of data across different locations.

Data providers upload their datasets into their Snowflake accounts within the Snowflake Marketplace for the purpose of data sharing and secure exchange. Subsequently, these datasets are securely distributed to data consumers via the platform. Snowflake employs strong encryption and access control measures to guarantee the confidentiality and protection of data during its transmission and storage.

The metadata catalog is an essential element of the Marketplace architecture. The catalog contains comprehensive data regarding the datasets accessible on the site, encompassing descriptions, usage policies, and pricing details. Users can search and explore datasets by utilizing this metadata. After a data consumer selects a dataset they are interested in, Snowflake's design enables effortless integration of the external data into their existing Snowflake data warehouse. This integration is crucial for guaranteeing that the data can be easily utilized in analytics and reporting.

Data providers might choose to generate revenue from their datasets by establishing price and licensing conditions for their data. The platform has usage tracking and reporting methods, allowing data producers to monitor the utilization of their datasets and make income appropriately.

Snowflake's architecture is specifically built to achieve exceptional scalability and performance. It utilizes the capabilities of distributed computing to effectively process intricate queries, guaranteeing that customers can retrieve and analyze extensive datasets from the Marketplace without sacrificing performance.

The Marketplace architecture is in accordance with Snowflake's robust governance and compliance standards. It guarantees that the sharing of data adheres to regulations and enables companies to retain authority over their data assets.

The design of the Snowflake Marketplace includes key features such as a cloud-native infrastructure, a secure data exchange system, a metadata catalog, integration capabilities, and strong scalability. This architectural design allows businesses to effectively utilize external data while maintaining strict adherence to security and governance norms. Snowflake's Marketplace architecture is strategically designed to cater to the changing requirements of both data providers and consumers, as data sharing and monetization remain crucial aspects of the data landscape.

Data Discovery and Search

Data Discovery and Search are crucial components of the Snowflake Marketplace, enabling data consumers to easily discover and utilize the extensive collection of datasets available. Users may effectively navigate, discover, and assess datasets that correspond to their precise analytical requirements.

The core of Data Discovery and Search is a metadata catalog that holds extensive information about the datasets accessible in the marketplace. The catalog contains metadata, which encompasses dataset descriptions, data source details, licensing conditions, pricing, and usage regulations.

Snowflake offers customers advanced search capabilities, enabling them to narrow down and enhance their search queries by using different parameters for filtering and refining. Users can perform searches based on keywords, data sources, industry, data format, and other criteria. This feature guarantees that users may precisely identify the specific datasets they need.

Data Discovery frequently incorporates data preview functionalities, allowing users to obtain a peek at the dataset's contents before deciding whether to obtain it. This feature is essential for evaluating the quality, pertinence, and appropriateness of data for particular analytical tasks.

Metadata enrichment is enhancing the metadata of each dataset to provide valuable insights. This involves incorporating appropriate tags, categories, and classifications into datasets, hence enhancing their discoverability according to user preferences.

Certain Marketplaces include user-generated evaluations and rankings. The inclusion of this social component enables data consumers to leverage the insights and evaluations of their peers, enhancing the decision-making process.

Snowflake's Marketplace is closely integrated with data integration and ETL (Extract, Transform, Load) solutions. The link enables customers to effortlessly import certain datasets into their Snowflake data warehouse, streamlining the data-collecting procedure.

Data profiling encompasses the ability to analyze and understand the composition, integrity, and attributes of a given dataset. This information assists data consumers in evaluating whether the dataset fulfills their unique criteria.

The metadata of each dataset contains comprehensive details regarding licensing terms, compliance obligations, and any limitations on data utilization. This guarantees that users possess complete knowledge of their responsibilities and entitlements while utilizing the data.

The inclusion of Data Discovery and Search features in the Snowflake Marketplace greatly improves the ease of access and usefulness of datasets for individuals who consume data. This feature not only reduces the time and effort required to locate relevant data, but also encourages decision-making based on data by ensuring that users can access the most suitable and reliable datasets.

Snowflake's Data Discovery and Search features enable enterprises to effectively explore the Marketplace, identify valuable datasets, and make well-informed decisions regarding data acquisition. Snowflake facilitates the efficient exploration of data by simplifying the process and offering comprehensive metadata and preview capabilities. This empowers data consumers to confidently and effortlessly leverage external data resources.

Data Listing and Publication

The process of listing and publishing data in Snowflake's Marketplace is a methodical and user-friendly procedure that allows data producers to share their datasets with a worldwide audience of potential customers. This functionality is crucial in broadening the scope of valuable data assets, facilitating data monetization endeavors, and promoting collaboration within the Snowflake ecosystem.

The process commences with data suppliers preparing their datasets for inclusion. This entails verifying that the data is in the correct format, is free of errors, and includes the essential metadata, descriptions, and tags. Data that has been thoroughly produced is more inclined to appeal to prospective consumers.

Data providers generate comprehensive metadata for their datasets during the process of metadata creation. This metadata contains crucial details, such as the origin of the data, a description of the data, policies on how it can be used, pricing information, and any related paperwork. Metadata is essential for aiding data consumers in the discovery and comprehension of available datasets.

Data providers customize the settings for their datasets within the Snowflake platform. In this step, it is necessary to define the pricing models, licensing conditions, and access controls. Data providers have the option to decide whether they want to distribute their data for free or monetize it. They can also establish licensing agreements that are in line with their objectives for sharing data.

After configuring and preparing the listing, data providers can publish their datasets to the Snowflake Marketplace. Snowflake guarantees the secure dissemination of data by strictly following rigorous data privacy and security regulations.

Data consumers can now utilize a range of filters, such as industry, domain, or dataset type, to search and explore datasets on the Marketplace. The comprehensive metadata offered by data suppliers assists consumers in locating the most pertinent datasets for their requirements. Users can preview datasets and gain a comprehensive understanding of their content and cost before making a selection. Snowflake enables the secure transfer and integration of selected datasets into the user's Snowflake account.

Snowflake's Marketplace architecture incorporates capabilities for tracking and reporting consumption. These tools facilitate data providers in monitoring the utilization of their datasets and generating financial reports depending on data usage.

Data consumers are given the opportunity to offer comments and ratings for the datasets they access. This feature promotes a cooperative atmosphere and enhances the overall caliber of the datasets that are listed.

Data listing and publication in the Snowflake Marketplace enable a mutually beneficial situation for both data sources and users. Providers can access other sources of income, broaden the scope of their data, and obtain valuable information about how data is being utilized. Simultaneously, users can obtain a wide array of top-notch datasets, which promotes innovation and facilitates decision-making based on data.

Snowflake's Marketplace is a platform that enables businesses to share and monetize data. It offers a fast and safe method for listing and publishing data.

The Snowflake Marketplace allows suppliers to profit from their data and applications by making them available to Snowflake users. It is essential for suppliers to implement successful monetization strategies to increase income and take advantage of the increasing demand for data-driven solutions in the Snowflake ecosystem.

Vendors have the option to implement a subscription-based pricing plan, allowing users to pay a regular charge to use their data or application on Snowflake Marketplace. This strategy provides vendors with consistent revenue streams and enables users to manage their spending efficiently.

Implementing a pay-per-use pricing model charges users based on their data or application consumption. This adaptable pricing strategy adjusts rates based on the amount of data used, appealing to consumers with different data consumption requirements.

Vendors can provide tiered pricing plans that offer varying levels of features, functions, and usage constraints. This method addresses the varied requirements of users and enables vendors to benefit from both small-scale and enterprise customers. Vendors can utilize upselling and cross-selling tactics to enhance their income opportunities. This is providing extra features, premium services, or related items to current consumers to increase their average revenue per user (ARPU).

Vendors can also generate revenue by offering customization services, adapting their data or program to suit the unique requirements of particular consumers or organizations. Providing professional services such as advising, training, and implementation support can generate extra income and improve client satisfaction.

Collaborating with other vendors or service providers in the Snowflake ecosystem through partnerships and alliances might lead to revenue sharing and collaborative offerings. Vendors can tap into new markets, broaden their consumer base, and generate extra cash by utilizing partnerships and alliances.

Value-based Pricing includes setting prices based on the perceived value that consumers attribute to the data or application. Vendors can justify higher prices and increase their market share by showing the concrete benefits and return on investment of their products.

Vendors must implement efficient monetization techniques to fully utilize Snowflake Marketplace and optimize revenue generation. Vendors can achieve sustained development and success within the Snowflake ecosystem by using creative pricing strategies, utilizing partnerships, and prioritizing value delivery to customers.

Prerequisite for Listing on Marketplace

To list data or apps on the Snowflake Marketplace, several conditions and qualifications must be met to guarantee quality, stability, and compliance with Snowflake's platform. Vendors can improve their visibility in the marketplace by comprehending these standards and preparing their offerings accordingly for submission

Prerequisites:

- Verify that the data or application is compatible with Snowflake's platform, including its data formats, query syntax, and security standards.
- Perform comprehensive testing to verify that the data or application adheres to high-quality requirements, encompassing correctness, performance, and reliability.
- Documentation should be thorough and detailed, covering the functionality, usage instructions, and needs of the data or program. The documentation should be unambiguous, succinct, and readily available to users.
- Ensure security compliance by implementing strong security measures to safeguard user data and adhere to Snowflake's security standards and regulations, including encryption, access limits, and data masking.
- Verify that the data or application has appropriate license agreements and does not violate any intellectual property rights.
- Scalability involves designing the data or application in a way that enables it to manage growing amounts of data or users without compromising performance or stability.

Qualifications:

- Make sure the data or application serves a pertinent business requirement or use case in the Snowflake ecosystem, including analytics, data warehousing, or data integration.
- Show originality and distinctiveness in the data or application's characteristics, functionality, or technology stack in comparison to current offers in the market.
- Clearly state the benefits of the data or application for Snowflake users, emphasizing how it can enhance their data analytics or operations.

- Present proof of customer success stories or testimonials that demonstrate the efficacy and influence of the data or application in practical situations.
- Commit to providing continuous support and maintenance for the data or program, which includes bug fixes, updates, and client assistance.

Meeting the specified conditions and qualifications is crucial for listing data or applications on the Snowflake Marketplace. Vendors can improve the visibility, credibility, and adoption of their solutions within the Snowflake

Conclusion

This chapter offers a thorough analysis of this innovative platform that has revolutionized the way organizations obtain, exchange, and profit from data. It provides an introduction to Snowflake's Marketplace, highlighting its crucial function in enabling the sharing and collaboration of data, and emphasizes the benefits it provides to both data producers and consumers.

The chapter also explains the underlying architecture that drives the functionality of the Marketplace. It elucidates how Snowflake's cloud-native infrastructure, multi-cluster deployment, and stringent security measures guarantee the secure and efficient transmission of data within the ecosystem.

This chapter provides a detailed explanation of the organized procedure for creating and sharing data lists. It emphasizes the significance of data preparation, metadata generation, listing setup, and secure data dissemination. This technique enables data producers to access a worldwide audience and generate revenue from their datasets while retaining control over access and license terms.

In summary, the chapter offers a comprehensive comprehension of Snowflake's Marketplace, encompassing its structure as well as its practical elements such as data exploration, listing, and dissemination. This platform demonstrates how it has revolutionized the data ecosystem by enabling enterprises to efficiently interact, share, and utilize data resources in a secure and efficient manner.

In the next chapter, we will explore Snowpark, a component of the Snowflake data platform that effortlessly integrates robust programming capabilities into Snowflake. The tool enables users to perform intricate data transformations, analytics, and data engineering tasks in Snowflake by providing the ability to write custom code in familiar programming languages.

CHAPTER 10
Snowpark

Introduction

The Snowpark component of the Snowflake data platform seamlessly incorporates powerful programming capabilities within Snowflake. It facilitates complex data transformations, analytics, and data engineering tasks in Snowflake by allowing users to write custom code in programming languages they are acquainted with.

Snowpark enhances Snowflake's capabilities by enabling effortless and integrated programming. Users can construct advanced data processing algorithms within Snowflake, reducing the necessity for other tools or intricate data pipelines.

Snowpark supports many programming languages such as Java, Scala, and JavaScript. Users can choose the language that best suits their requirements and interests. The presence of well-known programming languages enables developers and data architects to easily switch to Snowpark and effectively utilize their current expertise.

The Snowpark development environment offers crucial tools and resources for authoring, validating, and deploying Snowpark code within the Snowflake platform. It encompasses code editors, debugging functionalities, and integration with Snowflake's data processing engines. The development environment allows users to create powerful data transformations and analytics workflows, ensuring a seamless and effective development process.

Snowflake enhances its capabilities as a comprehensive data platform with the introduction of Snowpark. The support for several programming languages and the dedicated development environment of Snowpark offer customers the essential flexibility and tools to optimize the potential of their data within Snowflake. Snowpark allows enterprises to utilize their programming expertise to create intricate data processing logic within Snowflake, resulting in streamlined data workflows and expedited data-driven insights.

Structure

In this chapter, the following topics will be covered:

- Snowpark Programming Languages
- Snowpark Development Environment
- Best Practices to be Followed While Using Snowpark

Snowpark Programming Languages

Snowflake's Snowpark is an innovative addition that enhances the data processing capabilities of the Snowflake Data Cloud. It enables data engineers, data scientists, and developers to create and execute complex data transformations and computations in Snowflake using programming languages and tools that they are already familiar with. This section will examine the fundamental nature of Snowpark, its essential elements, its advantages, and its influence on data processing and analytics.

The purpose of Snowpark is to address conventional constraints in data processing within the Snowflake platform. Snowflake's SQL-based method is optimized for structured data, whereas Snowpark caters to the demand for versatile, customizable, and expressive processing choices for semi-structured and unstructured data.

Snowpark is a novel and robust programming language introduced by Snowflake. This language is based on commonly employed programming ideas and is specifically crafted to operate flawlessly within Snowflake. Developers can utilize this tool to design intricate data transformations, calculations, and bespoke logic in a manner that is both familiar and fast.

The Snowpark Runtime refers to a collection of services and resources in Snowflake that facilitate the execution of Snowpark Language code. It comprises the Snowpark Engine, which builds and executes Snowpark code with high efficiency and security, and the Snowpark Function Library, a compilation of pre-existing functions designed for typical data processing operations.

Snowpark is specifically built to smoothly connect with widely used programming tools and frameworks such as Java, Python, and Scala. Developers can utilize their current expertise and software collections to improve data processing capabilities within Snowflake.

Advantages of Snowflake's Snowpark

- Snowpark introduces a novel programming language that offers enhanced flexibility and expressiveness in data processing, surpassing the limitations of conventional SQL. This is especially advantageous when working with semi-structured or unstructured data sources such as JSON, XML, and Parquet.
- Developers can utilize their pre-existing proficiency in programming languages such as Java, Python, or Scala to construct intricate data conversions and analytics. Consequently, this results in heightened efficiency and reduced timeframes for development.
- Snowpark facilitates the smooth incorporation of other libraries and tools, empowering data engineers and data scientists to utilize their chosen frameworks for activities such as machine learning, data preparation, and customized data processing.
- Snowpark enhances the integration of data processing and analytics within Snowflake, hence fostering a cohesive data platform. Data engineers, data scientists, and analysts can enhance their collaborative efforts and streamline the sharing of information.

The capabilities of Snowpark enable a diverse array of use cases, facilitating the creation of intricate data conversions for various data types. It is especially advantageous for managing semi-structured data forms. Snowpark enables data engineers to enhance data by integrating it with external sources, web services, or machine learning models.

Data scientists can construct personalized analytics and machine learning pipelines using their preferred programming languages and libraries. Real-time processing refers to the ability to process data and deliver results immediately, without any delay or latency.

Developers can utilize Snowpark to enhance real-time data processing situations, such as monitoring, alerting, and dynamic data enrichment.

Effects on Data Processing and Analytics

The introduction of Snowpark marks a notable advancement in Snowflake's capabilities, resulting in a considerable influence on data processing and analytics.

Snowpark enables data engineers and data scientists to quickly create and refine data processing and analytics processes, thereby lowering the time required to gain valuable insights for important business choices. It facilitates collaboration between data engineering and data science teams by offering a consolidated platform for data processing and analytics, resulting in improved cross-functional efficiency.

Snowflake's inherent data governance capabilities encompass Snowpark, ensuring that data processing operations adhere to security and compliance protocols. Snowpark benefits from Snowflake's scalability, enabling it to manage and process enormous volumes of data efficiently without compromising performance, even under increasing demands or workloads.

Snowpark offers comprehensive assistance for machine learning (ML) tasks by facilitating the smooth integration of ML frameworks and libraries into the Snowflake platform. This allows data engineers and data scientists to utilize their preferred machine learning tools directly within Snowflake, avoiding the necessity of transferring data across various systems and settings.

Snowpark enhances ML workflows by providing built-in compatibility with widely used programming languages such as Scala and Java, enabling users to develop personalized ML algorithms and manipulate data using familiar syntax and libraries. The flexibility of machine learning allows practitioners to make use of their current skills and libraries, which speeds up the development process and enhances productivity.

In addition, the integration of Snowpark with Snowflake's data processing capabilities guarantees exceptional performance and scalability for machine learning applications. By utilizing Snowflake's distributed computing architecture, users can effectively process extensive datasets and perform intricate machine learning algorithms. This leads to expedited generation of insights and enhanced decision-making capabilities.

Snowflake's Snowpark is an innovative addition to the Snowflake Data Cloud, enabling enterprises to fully leverage the capabilities of their data. Snowflake is a comprehensive data platform that offers flexible and expressive programming capabilities, seamless connection with external tools, and support for complicated data processing use cases. It is designed to meet the modern data engineering and analytics needs. With the increasing importance of data as a valuable resource for enterprises, Snowpark is positioned to have a crucial impact on promoting innovation, adaptability, and making decisions based on data.

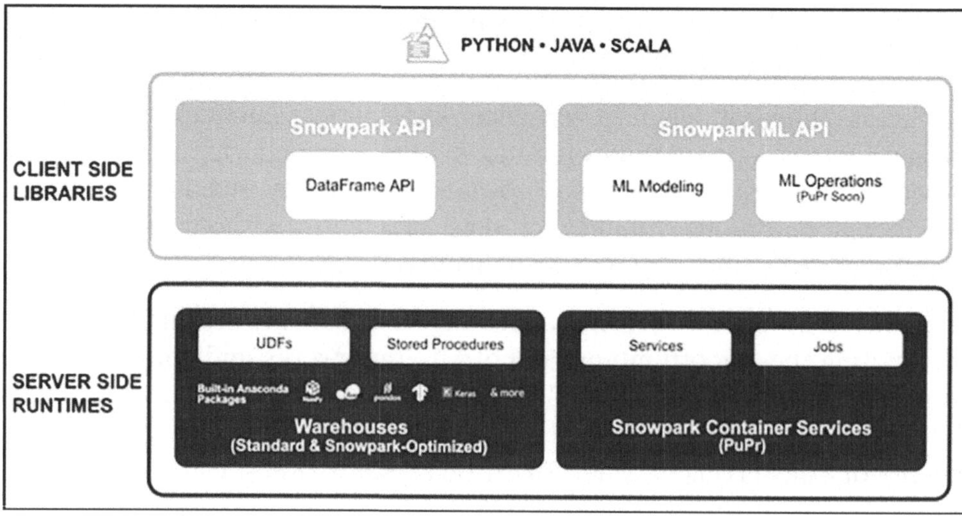

***Figure 10.1**: Snowpark Hierarchy (Source: https://www.snowflake.com/en/data-cloud/snowpark/)*

Snowpark Development Environment

The Snowpark Development Environment is an essential element of Snowflake's Snowpark functionality. It enables data engineers, data scientists, and developers to create and execute sophisticated data transformations and computations using well-known programming languages within the Snowflake Data Cloud. This section will provide an in-depth analysis of the Snowpark Development Environment, examining its essential characteristics, advantages, and contribution to improving data transformation and analytics capabilities.

The Snowpark Development Environment is a specialized workspace in Snowflake that is used for the development, testing, and execution of Snowpark Language code. The platform offers a cooperative and unified setting where data experts can effortlessly generate, modify, and run Snowpark scripts.

Key features of the Snowpark Development Environment

Snowpark offers an integrated development environment (IDE) that facilitates the use of widely used programming languages such as Java, Python, and Scala. This IDE enables developers to write and debug code with high efficiency, utilizing features such as code auto-completion and syntax highlighting.

The environment includes integrated version control methods, which enable teams to efficiently maintain and communicate on Snowpark code. This guarantees that modifications to the code are monitored, documented, and assigned a version number, thus improving the development process. The Development Environment allows users to directly execute Snowpark scripts, enabling real-time testing and validation of code logic and data manipulations.

Snowpark Development Environment effortlessly incorporates Snowflake's services and resources, such as Snowflake Data Cloud, Snowpark Runtime, and Snowflake Function Library. This integration guarantees a seamless shift from the development phase to the deployment phase.

Snowpark boosts developer productivity by offering a dedicated workstation equipped with an integrated development environment, hence improving efficiency and output. Developers can enhance their productivity by writing, testing, and debugging code more effectively, hence shortening development cycles. Teams can work together on Snowpark projects in a shared setting. The integration of version control and collaboration capabilities facilitates the efficient coordination of team efforts and the sharing of code.

The capability to run Snowpark scripts instantly enables prompt testing and verification of code modifications. This expedites the processes of development and troubleshooting. The Snowpark Development Environment smoothly combines with Snowflake's wider ecosystem, guaranteeing a cohesive experience for data processing, analytics, and governance.

The Snowpark Development Environment is very adaptable and capable of accommodating a diverse array of use cases. Data engineers can utilize the platform to create and evaluate intricate data transformations, simplifying the process of preprocessing, cleansing, and altering data. Data scientists can utilize Snowpark to construct and verify personalized analytics and machine learning workflows using their choice of programming languages and frameworks.

Data enrichment involves the process of enhancing data by integrating it with external sources, web services, or machine learning models within the development environment. The ability to test data in real-time is highly important for jobs related to data validation, as it guarantees the quality and consistency of the data.

The Snowpark Development Environment significantly influences data translation and analytics processes. Developers can swiftly advance and refine data transformation and analytics workflows, hence decreasing the time required to gain valuable insights for crucial business determinations. The setting promotes collaboration among data experts, resulting in more effective teamwork and sharing of expertise.

Snowflake's strong data governance capabilities are also applicable to Snowpark, guaranteeing that development operations conform to security and compliance protocols. Snowpark leverages Snowflake's inherent scalability, allowing it to effectively manage and process extensive data transformation and analytics operations.

The Snowpark Development Environment revolutionizes the field of data transformation and analytics. The platform offers a specialized, unified, and cooperative environment for creating Snowpark code, allowing data engineers, data scientists, and developers to utilize their programming abilities within the Snowflake Data Cloud. The Snowflake platform empowers enterprises by improving efficiency, expediting development cycles, and promoting collaboration. This results in quicker insights and more informed decision-making.

The Snowpark-optimized warehouses in Snowflake offer customized computing resources specifically designed for Snowpark workloads, guaranteeing efficient execution of data processing and analytics tasks. These warehouses are designed to fulfill the precise needs of Snowpark jobs, maximizing performance and efficient use of resources for improved productivity and scalability.

Best Practices to be Followed While Using Snowpark

Snowpark enables users to enhance and tailor data processing and analytics workflows using well-known programming languages like Scala and Java. To properly utilize Snowpark, it is important to have a thorough awareness of its capabilities and to follow best practices to achieve efficient development and excellent performance:

- Prior to embarking on Snowpark development, it is essential to grasp the structure, application programming interfaces (APIs), and incorporation of Snowpark with Snowflake. Acquaint yourself with the documentation, tutorials, and sample code of Snowpark to obtain a comprehensive understanding of how to use it and its possibilities.
- Commence with modest endeavors. Initiate your journey by exploring uncomplicated scenarios and progressively escalate intricacy as you enhance your expertise in Snowpark. Commencing with smaller tasks facilitates the gradual acquisition of knowledge and mitigates the likelihood of facing difficulties in more extensive endeavors.

- Make use of integrated development environments (IDEs) and development tools that provide support for Scala and Java programming. Integrated Development Environments (IDEs) such as IntelliJ IDEA or Visual Studio Code offer functionalities such as code completion, debugging, and syntax highlighting, which improve the whole development process.
- Adhere to established guidelines for crafting efficient and optimized code to guarantee maximum performance. This involves reducing needless data conversions, utilizing parallel processing, and optimizing resource allocation to maximize performance and minimize execution durations.
- Employ meticulous testing and debugging methodologies to promptly detect and rectify flaws at the initial stages of the development process. Employ unit tests, integration tests, and debugging tools to verify the functionality of code and detect possible bottlenecks or problems.
- Observe resource consumption and performance data to detect any performance bottlenecks or limitations in resources. Monitor the utilization of the CPU, RAM, and query execution times to optimize the allocation of resources and guarantee the efficient execution of Snowpark activities.
- Implement version control systems such as Git to efficiently manage code modifications, facilitate collaboration with team members, and accurately monitor project history. Version control enables the collaboration, rollback, and deployment of code, guaranteeing the integrity and maintainability of the code.
- Engage in continuous learning by participating in training sessions, webinars, and community forums to stay informed about the newest innovations and best practices in Snowpark development. Engaging in continuous learning allows you to utilize novel features and strategies to improve your proficiency in Snowpark creation.

Users can maximize the capabilities of Snowpark by adhering to these recommended methods. This will allow them to optimize speed, stimulate innovation, and expand Snowflake's capacities in data processing and analytics processes.

Conclusion

In summary, this chapter has offered a thorough examination of this groundbreaking aspect of Snowflake's Data Cloud. Snowpark is a groundbreaking advancement in the field of data transformation and analytics, providing a flexible platform for data engineers, data scientists, and developers. To summarize, let's review the main points covered in the chapter, which include an overview of

Snowpark, the programming languages used in Snowpark, and the development environment for Snowpark.

Snowpark is an innovative addition to Snowflake's ecosystem, specifically created to meet the increasing demand for adaptable and dynamic data processing capabilities. Users are enabled to utilize their programming talents in Snowflake, hence expanding opportunities for data transformation and analytics.

Snowpark introduces the Snowpark Language, a robust programming language familiar to proficient developers in Java, Python, and Scala. This programming language facilitates complex data manipulations, calculations, and personalized algorithms, empowering users to efficiently handle semi-structured and unstructured data.

The Snowpark Development Environment offers a collaborative workplace equipped with an integrated development environment, version control, script execution capabilities, and easy connection with Snowflake's services. It improves efficiency, fosters cooperation, allows for immediate testing, and ensures a seamless transition from development to deployment.

The influence of Snowpark on data transformation and analytics is significant. It expedites the process of developing cycles, decreases the time it takes to gain valuable insights, and promotes effective collaboration among data experts. Snowpark enables data engineers to handle intricate data transformations, empowers data scientists to construct customized analytics pipelines, and allows developers to enhance data – all inside a cohesive ecosystem.

In addition, Snowpark integrates smoothly with Snowflake's robust data governance and scalability capabilities, guaranteeing that data processing operations comply with security and compliance regulations while efficiently managing large-scale data processing workloads.

As enterprises become more aware of the significance of utilizing data as a strategic resource, Snowpark emerges as a crucial tool that enables them to fully exploit the capabilities of their data. It promotes innovation, adaptability, and decision-making based on data, making it an essential element of contemporary data engineering and analytics. Snowpark empowers enterprises to effectively address the dynamic challenges and possibilities presented by the data ecosystem.

Index

D

M

O

Q

R

S